How We Feel

An Insight into the Emotional World of Teenagers

of related interest

Children in Charge
The Child's Right to a Fair Hearing
Edited by Mary John
ISBN 1 85302 368 X
Children in Charge 1

Children in Our Charge
The Child's Right to Resources
Edited by Mary John
ISBN 1 85302 369 8
Children in Charge 2

A Charge Against Society
The Child's Right to Protection
Edited by Mary John
ISBN 1 85302 411 2
Children in Charge 3

How We Feel

An Insight into the Emotional World of Teenagers

Edited by Jacki Gordon and Gillian Grant
Foreword by Peter Wilson

Jessica Kingsley Publishers
London and Bristol, Pennsylvania

First published in the United Kingdom in 1997 by
Jessica Kingsley Publishers Ltd
116 Pentonville Road
London N1 9JB, England
and
1900 Frost Road, Suite 101
Bristol, PA 19007, U S A

Copyright © 1997 the Health Promotion Department,
Greater Glasgow Health Board and the publisher

Foreword copyright © 1997 Peter Wilson

Library of Congress Cataloging in Publication Data
A CIP catalogue record for this book is available from the Library of Congress

British Library Cataloguing in Publication Data
A CIP catalogue record for this book is available from the British Library

ISBN 1 85302 439 2

Printed and Bound in Great Britain by
Athenaeum Press, Gateshead, Tyne and Wear

Contents

To the young people who gave us the privilege of glimpsing into their emotional worlds – we hope this book does you justice.

Acknowledgements

This book would not have been possible without the funding and support of The Health Promotion Department, Greater Glasgow Health Board.

There a number of individuals who deserve special thanks for advice, practical and emotional support, and chocolate: John Abbot, Paul Barclay, Avril Blamey, Janice Boyle, Graham Bryce, Sally Butler, Jan Cassidy, Lisa Cohen, John Crawford, Sharon Dougan, Xanthe Fry, Ann-Marie Gillen, Ron and Evelyn Grant, Susan Grant, Marcus Gray, Inez Gribben, Norma Greenwood, Timothy Gordon, Fiona Hamilton, Anne Houston, Ruth Kendall, Angela King, Frances MacDonald, Susan McGinnis, Margaret McGranachan, Paul McLean, Jackie McNally, Eddie McMillan, Trevor Lakey, Elaine Moffat, Kenny and Norma Morrison, Craig Mowat and the rest of the Mowat clan, Honour O'Brien, George Potter, Alistair Ramsay, Lorna Renwick, Joan and Peter Rodney, Philip and Cherie Rodney, Jac Ross, Mary Ross, Jenny Secker, Judy Tait, Carol Tannahill, Andy Thornton, Patrick West, Peter Wilson, Phil Wilson, the Youth Team, the staff at the participating schools, the pupils of Shawlands Academy who produced the illustrations for this book, and the rest of our families and friends who have put up with Howie Feel for so long.

The views expressed in this book are those of the authors and of young people in Glasgow and do not necessarily represent those of their employing organisations.

Foreword

There can be no doubt that the mental health of young people is of crucial importance, not only to their everyday experiences but also to their general growth and development, and readiness and capacity to enter into the adult world. It is difficult, the more we think about it, to imagine anything more important, and yet it is a subject that, until recently, has been consistently overlooked, poorly understood and, as far as services are concerned, seriously underfunded. Mental health is a difficult concept; what we basically mean by it is emotional well-being, but there is a great deal of confusion about the term and all too frequently it is immediately confused with its opposite – that is to say mental illness. There is, in fact, an extensive literature on mental illness and mental disorder and a well-considered set of classifications that help to differentiate and understand people with serious mental health problems. This is very much within the domain of clinical and academic psychiatry and undoubtedly serves a useful purpose. However it does not adequately attend to the issue of health or enable us to take into account the wide and complex variations that exist within the broad spectrum of what can generally be called the mentally healthy. It is clear that young people grow up very differently and deal with the pressures of their lives in a variety of ways according to their own personalities and temperaments, their family backgrounds and socio-economic circumstances.

We need to know much more about what it is that constitutes mental health and what we mean by the term. There has been a growing interest in the subject amongst mental health professionals and those concerned with the promotion of mental health. The NHS Health Advisory Service (1995) publication *Together We Stand*, for example, sets out its agendas with a definition of mental health. This essentially lists a number of key capacities: to develop psychologically, emotionally, intellectually and spiritually; to initiate and sustain mutually satisfying personal relationships; to become aware of others and empathise with them; to use psychological distress as a developmental process so that it does not hinder or impair further development.

All of this is helpful, but the question remains: what does it actually feel like to be a young person in the midst of developing these vital capacities? From the fields of psychology and psychoanalysis we know a fair bit about the core developmental anxieties of adolescence; of adjusting to the impact of puberty and establishing a separate identity. We know that each individual has his or her own idiosyncratic pathway through adolescence, balancing the pressures of the external world with the influences of past and present experience, and that throughout, the issue is how to live, how to develop and give expression to potentiality and how to be assertive and establish dignity and self-worth. But we don't know enough – or we too easily move out of listening distance – about how all of this is experienced by the young people themselves. We need constantly to keep in touch with their perspective as they live their adolescence so that we might better understand and care. *How We Feel* is a much needed and welcome book – for, through its comprehensive study and diary accounts, it provides an invaluable insight into young people as they grow and encounter the demands of their present and future worlds. Here we have a vivid picture of the variety and complexity of their emotional experience. Most positively, there is much that gives a clear sense of what it feels like for some young people to feel healthy, to feel good and joyful, on top of the world, unafraid to face its challenges, and enjoy a 'good laugh'. There is fun and levity in this, as well as seriousness and a determined purpose to master new experiences, to find out and learn. This is healthy living, maybe at its best, and there can be no doubt that the young people themselves know what it is that can make for this good life. Stimulating school experiences count a great deal, as do supportive families, but, perhaps most important of all, are friends.

At the same time, both within those that are making such ready and confident progress but more predominantly in those less sure of their abilities, there is a great sense of pressure and distress, which, in varying degrees, is an inherent part of the developmental process. The strain of exams, the expectations of parents and the tensions of friendships all add to a sense of inevitable conflict and dissatisfaction, however temporary, that has to be constantly dealt with. There is for many – some more extremely than others – a deep sense of hurt, betrayal and injustice in being excluded or used or insufficiently acknowledged or loved. There are often intense frightening feelings that may find outward expression in angry, violent behaviour but not infrequently leave the young person feeling a great deal of self-hatred with suicidal thoughts.

The breadth and intensity of feelings that emerge from this book, as expressed so simply and directly by the young people themselves, is both exhilarating and alarming to all concerned, not least to themselves. What comes through so clearly are young human beings discovering their emergent adult lives, as distinct from their parents, for themselves to own and do with as they would wish. And in this process of discovery there is a growing recognition of other people's differences, vulnerabilities and weaknesses and of their own complexities and contradictions. This, perhaps, lies at the heart of the adolescent experience: the perplexing coincidence of so many different states and sensations. One young person says it quite clearly:

> Some days I feel trapped. Homework sometimes gets on top of me, but I still find a way to do it. Some days I feel great, I play football and if I am lucky I score a goal, and sometimes I just cannot be bothered. Some days school is great and it goes in fast. Some days it's rubbish and very, very, very slow. Some days the teachers seem to be on your back and other days they help you a lot. Some days I am angry at my sisters and some days I don't annoy them.

Another comments more briefly: 'Today I don't know how I feel. I change every five minutes, my life is very weird'. And again: 'I feel quite depressed, but happy today'. It is not surprising that someone should reflect: 'I keep on asking myself questions and wondering if I am normal or not'.

What is so valuable about this book is that it presents us with a kaleidoscope of statements and images that captures the ordinary richness of the adolescent experience. With all this in mind, it can then attend to the many issues that arise about gender differences, about questions of what is and what is not normal, about the role of the GP and other professionals and about the importance of parenting, education and health promotion. With the voices of the young people themselves in our ear, the more able are we, with them, to provide the facilities and help they need.

Peter Wilson
Director of Young Minds

Preface

Let us stop for a minute to reflect on the ways in which how we feel about our lives impacts on our behaviour, our hopes and experiences, and the reactions of others to us. If we do this we cannot help but recognise the central impact of our emotional worlds on our current and future well-being and quality of life, and on our interactions with other people. In short, our feelings and emotions are not only integral to our state of health but also affect many of the influences on our health.

Health has several dimensions – physical, mental, social and spiritual – and is not a fixed or absolute state. Rather, health is created in daily lives, being affected by our own actions, those of other people and the environments in which we live and work. In acknowledging this, we also need to acknowledge our responsibilities – not only in relation to our own health but also as contributors to the health of the many other people on whom our actions impact.

The focus of this book is on adolescent mental health, on how this is created and can be enhanced. It places the views and feelings of young people at the centre of this analysis and reflects on their implications for the many agencies with a role to play in promoting the mental health of young people. In doing so the book importantly sheds a new light on adolescent mental health and its promotion.

The first section of the book reports the findings of an innovative survey carried out in secondary schools throughout Glasgow to paint a picture of the emotional health of a cross-section of young people in the city on one particular day in 1995. The purpose of the study was to give young people a mechanism to express, in their own words, how they were really feeling that day and to describe the influences (both positive and negative) on those feelings. The study was called Howie Feel because it recognised the importance of How We Feel.

In its later chapters the book brings in the views of professionals from a range of disciplines, but all with the common interest of promoting the mental health of young people. Their reflections on the implications of the Howie Feel data set are hugely challenging and inspiring. The views of young people are seen to be valid and important and, if our service responses are to be truly supportive to adolescents, we need to use these views to inform our work.

The city of Glasgow has a strong tradition of bringing local people together with professionals and workers from different agencies to develop co-ordinated action to achieve Health for All. This book contributes to that tradition and is an important component of our overall strategy to raise awareness of adolescent mental health needs and to develop appropriate responses to these needs. Howie Feel has not been a research study without practical outputs. It has spawned new mental health promotion work within schools, in communities and with parents – all of this placing the emotional needs of adolescents at the core.

The promotion of the health of young people cannot be seen as a short-term challenge. It will require attention and investment from all of us over many years until it is so firmly built in to the consciousness of public and professionals alike that supportive actions are continually effected. I hope that this book contributes to the realisation of that vision.

Carol Tannahill
Director of Health Promotion
Greater Glasgow Health Board

CHAPTER 1

'Howie Feel' is Conceived

In the beginning

It all started in the office of our friend Andy. He heads a team who work with young people on a range of health issues and, more importantly, he has a coffee filter machine rather than a jar of instant. As we waited for our coffee, we started to debate how best we can address the emotional and mental health needs of teenagers. We were very aware of the statistics which reveal, for instance, the percentage of teenagers who are anorexic or depressed or attempting suicides. These figures are very sobering, yet they do not provide us with a full picture of adolescent mental health. They tell us nothing about the experience of the vast majority of teenagers, the ones who have not become so overwhelmed that they attract a clinical diagnosis. We felt that we should find out precisely how it feels to be a teenager growing up today. Surely the way to do this would be to listen to young people and find out how it feels to be in their shoes. We decided to take a snapshot of teenagers' feelings and emotions – 'A sort of day in the life of a teenager' as Andy put it.

'Women With a Mission', we knuckled down to finding a way to obtain this snapshot view of the emotional world of teenagers today. That was one-and-a-half years ago. At last we have surfaced from analysing the responses of the 1634 teenagers who provided us with their personal accounts.

Do we not already know the way teenagers are feeling? After all, we were all teenagers once. Being a teenager today, however, is likely to be different to the way it was 20, 30 or 40 years ago. Values, attitudes and behaviours are all changing. It follows then that we cannot just conjure up our own experiences as teenagers and assume that teenagers will feel pretty much the same way as we did at their age.

Adults' views of teenagers often tend to extremes. Some regard teenage years as halcyon times; a period in life free from 'real worries'. At the other extreme there is a pervasive anti-youth feeling, fuelled perhaps by the media, which paints the teenager as hedonistic and unruly with a casual disrespect for both people and property. Prejudicial viewpoints such as these may result in the emotional needs of young people being overlooked, trivialised or dismissed.

We can't say teenagers are like this, or like that. In fact the notion of one 'youth culture' is now being rejected. We must therefore move to a sophisticated level of understanding which recognises diversity and the uniqueness of individuals. That is not to say that there are no commonalities. We hoped that by asking young people to let us know how they feel we could create a rich and vibrant tapestry of their experiences, one which would reflect the individual voice but at the same time allow us to tease out common threads.

Recently we have witnessed moves to consult young people on matters regarding their welfare. For instance, article 12 of the United Nations Convention, the Children Act (1989) and the Children Scotland Act (1995) spell out young people's rights to be heard. These legislations do not give young people a monopoly on having a say, but rather attempt to integrate their views into a comprehensive picture of their welfare. Likewise, we wanted to find out what young people are feeling in order to inform and supplement what is already known about adolescent mental health.

The term 'adolescent mental health' refers to more than the absence of mental illness. For instance, mental health can be seen to embrace emotions such as feeling good or good about yourself, confident, fulfilled, challenged, etc. – all of which help us form and maintain healthy relationships with others. The banner of mental health also covers the flipside of these positive emotions: feeling low or bad about yourself, unconfident, unfulfilled, frustrated, stressed, etc. Whilst such feelings are not viewed as 'disorders' as such, they can still result in feelings of distress.

Whereas many studies on mental health tend to restrict their focus to problems, we have used a wide-angle lens to look at the broad range of emotions experienced by teenagers in general, not just those who are experiencing major difficulties. We have pulled together this book in recognition of the fact that everyone has a role to play in promoting their mental health, rather than this being the sole responsibility of health professionals. When we hear about the way teenagers feel, hopefully this will give us the insight into how we can best support them.

We obtained our picture of adolescent mental health by giving out questionnaires to pupils from a range of schools across many areas of Glasgow. We wanted these questionnaires to be be viewed as acceptable, user-friendly and non-threatening. In line with these aims, and playing on the words 'how we feel', we devised the cartoon character Howie Feel who featured on all questionnaires and, hopefully, helped us to convey a more human face of research.

Our Howie Feel questionnaires were completed on an anonymous basis by 1634 boys and girls aged between thirteen-and-a-half and fourteen-and-a-half years. The full details of how we did this are spelt out in Appendix 1 and a copy of the questionnaire is presented in Appendix 2.

In general, the questionnaire was designed to elicit teenagers' accounts and viewpoints in their own words. By this means we were able to capture the adolescent voice in a way which resonated with emotion – a quality which is missing in stark statistics.

A step into the unknown

As we ripped open the sealed envelopes which contained completed questionnaires, we were often extremely moved by what we read; at other times we were uplifted or entertained. The daunting task for us was how could we sort and group the responses in a meaningful manner. We have read and re-read the questionnaires on countless occasions and have been careful not to infer meaning if it is not explicit nor to impose our framework on what teenagers have said. Rather, we have tried to allow the results to speak for themselves.

After going through the questionnaires several times, we developed coding frames which incorporated all the main points made by the teenagers and then counted the numbers mentioning each of these points. When these coding frames failed to account for a number of recurring responses we went back through the data with additional codes so that we could be confident that none fell through the net. We grouped and counted responses falling into designated categories. In this way we were able to ensure that when we report the data, we are not reporting our *impressions*. Rather, we have addressed the data set in a systematic and rigorous fashion.

The accounts which we present are in the teenagers' own words. Mistakes in spelling have been changed however, so as not to detract from the *content* of what is being said. Often we feel that it is appropriate to show only part of an account. For instance, in the chapter looking at family life we isolate the section of accounts which are relevant to this area.

To protect the anonymity of the respondents we have either removed or changed the names of people they mention (for our own amusement, we have substituted these with names of our own families and friends). There are, however, a handful of accounts which we would have liked to include but have decided not to as the particular circumstances are so unusual and finely drawn that the anonymity of the respondent may be jeopardised.

Our Howie Feel questionnaires were filled out at the end of October 1995, to coincide with Scottish Mental Health Week. They were filled out by Glasgow teenagers when they were in school. These factors (the timing, the people, and the place) will inevitably have a bearing on the results which we obtained. However, in Anne Houston's chapter (15) we see that our findings are supported by the experience of ChildLine Scotland. It would therefore seem that the issues for teenagers in Glasgow are likely to be similar to those for teenagers in any other city in Britain.

Howie Feel provides many teenagers with a voice to say how they feel. However, what Howie Feel does not tell us are the views of those young people who were absent from school on the day the questionnaires were completed, or whose parents did not give written consent for them to participate.

Also missing from the survey is an ethnic perspective. Initially we had hoped to identify the experiences of different ethnic groups. However, we abandoned this aim following advice that it would be insensitive and divisive to ask teenagers to indicate this information on their questionnaires.

In our analysis we look at what teenagers say, and they say a lot. Their responses are anything between one word and a whole page, and cover everything from the mundane to the extreme. To present a true picture of Howie Feel we have attempted to incorporate this entire spectrum.

Clearly there is plenty which our young people do not say, and we are in no position to comment on the specific contents of this black hole. Some of these unspoken areas will likely be about issues which teenagers do not consider to be worthy of mention or which are not uppermost in their minds. Furthermore, although many teenagers divulge very personal details, others choose not to do so by writing 'I don't want to talk about it' or hint at some event or situation without describing it. For instance, one girl writes that she feels unhappy 'when I think about my past'.

How do teenagers respond to being asked about their feelings? We consider that over 99 per cent of the questionnaires provide us with accounts which we consider to be 'valid' or serious. We feel that less than 1 per cent are 'wind-ups', that is respondents who are fooling around and not taking the questionnaire seriously: 'The Queen came to visit me. I gave her tea with teddy bears with the best china.' All of the wind-ups come from boys. Later we will see evidence of very clear gender differences in the degree to which boys and girls share their feelings. We wonder now whether these wind-ups reflect a conscious desire by the boys to keep the lid firmly sealed on their feelings.

In the main, we feel that our questionnaire is an effective tool for gaining an insight into teenagers' views on their mental health. The fact that the questionnaires are filled in so fully reassures us that the the majority of our teenagers view the questionnaires as acceptable. Some also volunteer very direct (unsolicited) written feedback about how they feel about participating in our survey:

> School was boring as usual, but we done a Howie Feel questionnaire and it was good.

> I like this Howie Feel Day idea because I have been bottling things up lately and this has given me a chance to express my feelings. Thank you.

> This paper was good for me as I don't often get the chance to say how I feel.

Not everyone views the questionnaire so positively. Some (mostly boys) are sceptical about its value and our motives. We feel that their comments endorse the need for studies such as ours:

> Who cares about how we feel?

> Today I had to fill in a stupid questionnaire about how I feel…but who cares? It's only me.

> Are you the reader getting paid for this because why didn't you do something ages ago?

Why not indeed. The time has come to listen to what teenagers have to say, to listen to how they are feeling.

Are you sitting comfortably?

CHAPTER 2

Field of Words

How do we feel? OK? Fine? Not bad? A bit under the weather? If you ask somebody out of the blue to say how they feel, you often get a rather vague or woolly response. In our Howie Feel study we wanted teenagers to think about and report their feelings in a reflective and considered manner. To engage them in this task we needed to encourage them to consider a range of different *kinds* of emotions – both positive and negative.

When Howie was just a twinkle in our eyes, a colleague of ours, Xanthe, asked some groups of teenagers to think of any words which described the way they can feel. Most of the emotions suggested were negative. So teenagers said 'stressed' but they didn't say 'calm'; they said 'tired' but not 'lively'. We balanced each negative emotion with a positive counterpart (and vice versa). This gave us 46 words spanning a range of emotions, half of which were positive and half negative. These words were used to develop our 'Field of Words'. This is a widely-used technique which aims to focus people's thinking on a particular issue. All it involves is a page with lots of different words scattered over it and people are asked to mark those words which are appropriate for them. For our purposes, the Field of Words consisted of a range of emotions, and teenagers were asked to circle all those emotions which described the way they were feeling on the day on which they completed their questionnaire.

Which words do the teenagers circle? Well, we find that rather than polarising their emotions as either positive or negative, many describe themselves as experiencing emotions *across* the spectrum, positive through to negative. So teenagers could feel *happy, bored* and *stressed* for example. Some emotions are identified more frequently than others, however, with the most commonly circled ones being *fine, happy, fed up* and *bored*. (These emotions are circled by 41%, 40%, 38%, and 37% of respondents respectively). So overall, what conclusions can we draw? Are teenagers feeling okay or not? First, it is reassuring to find that 62 per cent say that they feel *happy* or *fine*. However, that is not to say that all is rosy, as the results reveal that the experience of

HOWIE FEEL

Sometimes adults do not know how it really feels to be your age. On these pages we are asking you questions about how you feel. There are no right or wrong answers because we are all different. You do not need to put your name on the paper. We just want you to think carefully about each question and answer them all.

Here are lots of words which describe different kinds of feelings. Please draw a circle around each word which describes how you are feeling today.

coping
31%

laid back
19%

trapped
8%

chirpy
18%

not coping
11%

energetic
26%

confused
12%

bored
37%

tense
14%

useless
8%

happy
40%

bad about
the future
9%

cheerful
31%

lively
29%

sensitive
8%

pleased
20%

confident
22%

disappointed
8%

angry
13%

lonely
19%

brave
12%

fine
41%

stressed
19%

smug
5%

important
7%

romantic
14%

scared
7%

jealous
8%

depressed
19%

bitter
7%

lucky
23%

shy
11%

ashamed
5%

loved
18%

calm
34%

strong
15%

failure
7%

successful
11%

on top
of the
world
16%

fed up
39%

frustrated
15%

unconfident
12%

frightened
5%

good about the future
20%

pleased with
myself
15%

Figure 2.1

positive feelings does not preclude the experience of negative ones – perhaps unsurprisingly, 55 per cent of the young people reveal that they are *bored* or *fed up*. What is striking too, is the frequency with which some more distressing negative emotions are circled. For instance, 19 per cent describe themselves as *depressed* and 19 per cent describe themselves as *stressed*. In fact, 29 per cent circle either *depressed* or *stressed* – a result that alerts us to the fact that, for many, adolescence is not an easy time.

Even less-commonly circled emotions make for serious consideration. We deliberated over whether we should include these, or would readers want to know more than just the most common responses? We feel that we should not glibly ignore or reject the less-commonly expressed emotions. For instance, the fact that 8.5 per cent describe themselves as *useless* may not seem worthy of attention at first glance. But when we consider that this means that, in a group of 12 teenagers, one teenager feels so badly about himself/herself to feel that the label 'useless' fits, perhaps the figure starts to take on more meaning. Similarly, although at face value the percentage may seem low, is it not really quite worrying that one in fourteen described themselves as a *failure*?

In Figure 2.1 we show the percentage of teenagers circling each emotion, and we urge you to look at it. However, what this table fails to reveal are the very clear gender differences which emerge. Although boys and girls experience the same emotions, the data suggest that they do so to different degrees.

The emotions most commonly identified by boys are *bored* (42%), *fine* (40%), and *fed up* (38%). The girls' top three emotions are *happy* (46%), *fine* (40%) and *fed up* (38%).

Conducting statistical analyses[1] on the data, we find that boys are significantly more likely than girls to describe themselves as feeling:

laid-back	*bored*	*lucky*
smug	*confident*	*strong*
successful	*pleased with myself*	*bitter*

Conversely, girls are more likely than boys to describe themselves in the following ways:

happy	*unconfident*	*depressed*
cheerful	*confused*	*loved*
chirpy	*jealous*	*sensitive*
lively		

From these data, we see that boys feel (or at least describe themselves as feeling) more confident than do girls. We are reassured that this is not an artefact: the

---

1   We performed Chi-Square tests on the data (two-tailed, 1 d.f.). Where gender differences are quoted, significance is obtained at $p<0.01$, except for the emotions 'confident', 'unconfident', 'confused' and 'bitter', which are significant at $p<0.05$.

data are consistent and we see a clustering of *related* emotions which girls use and which boys use to describe themselves. So, for boys, we see that not only are they more likely than girls to describe themselves as *confident* but also as *pleased with myself, smug* and *successful.* Girls, on the other hand, are more likely to describe themselves not only as *unconfident* but also as *confused.* These findings give us our first glimpse of the tendency for more boys than girls to report that they feel good about themselves – an issue which is covered in more depth in Chapter 7.

When we look at the other gender differences we see that the girls' list includes many kinds of mood: *happy, chirpy, lively, sensitive* and *depressed.* It would seem that girls are more likely to describe themselves as experiencing strong emotions – highs and lows. Of particular interest is the fact that more girls than boys describe themselves as feeling depressed. Whilst it will not be the case that all these girls are depressed according to clinical criteria, the gender difference we see here is in line with what we know about the differential rates of depression in teenage girls and boys. Although pre-pubescent boys and girls experience depression to roughly the same extent, the rate in girls is higher following puberty and, by the age of about 15 or 16 years, it is twice as high amongst girls as compared with boys. This is probably because girls become more emotionally involved in their relationships with others and invest more emotion in other aspects of their lives (Graham and Hughes 1995). The fact that more girls than boys describe themselves as *sensitive* reinforces this point. Whilst the term 'sensitive' can be interpreted in very different ways (for example, touchy or empathic), a sense of responsiveness underpins all meanings of the word. In subsequent chapters we will see evidence of girls' inclination to engage at an emotional level with other people more frequently than is the case with boys.

Turning to the boys, we see that they are more likely than girls to circle *bored* and *laid back.* Again, this seems consistent with the view that girls engage at a more emotional level with different aspects of their lives. We also see that boys are more likely than girls to circle *strong,* but we don't know how they are interpreting this – do they mean physically or emotionally? We regret that here our questionnaire was rather less than perfect.

Before we leave this chapter, it is important to stress not only the differences between boys and girls but also the similarities. Each and every emotion in the Field of Words is circled by some boys and by some girls, and therefore any difference is one of *degree.* Furthermore, there are many emotions for which no gender difference is discernable, and some of these may challenge stereotypical notions. Boys and girls are equally likely to describe themselves as *shy,* as *angry* and as *romantic.*

Figure 2.2   *Tormod Smith*

CHAPTER 3

Happiness and Unhappiness

In the middle section of the questionnaire, young people were given the chance to let us know what sorts of factors influence their feelings. The questions were deliberately left open so that the things which were most important to the young people on that day could be recorded; we felt that we did not want to constrain or influence responses by presenting a list of things which the young people ticked or circled. When we interpret the results we have to bear these points in mind. Because teenagers could give any response, there are an infinite number of possibilities. It follows that the numbers giving a particular 'answer' are likely to be far smaller than if we had asked them to select a response from a range of options. Furthermore, because we did not constrain the teenagers in how they completed their questionnaires, it is likely that those issues which emerge are likely to be those which are most *salient* for them.

The following three chapters give a feel for the kind of information we got from the responses to the seven questions in the middle section of the questionnaire. We will go through the questions as they appeared on the questionnaire (see Appendix 2 for a full copy). We feel that this is the best way to present the findings and gives a good insight into the way the young people take to the task in hand. At this stage we will not reflect too much on the issues arising as these will be picked up in the 'Dear Diary' chapters, as well as in the chapters from those working in the field of adolescence.

We have chosen to summarise the main themes that come up for each question, while at the same time illustrating with quotes from the young people those issues which are both common and not so common. We came across a fair amount of overlap in the themes or issues which surface. To provide a 'feel' for the relative frequency with which issues arise, we have presented percentages for frequently occurring themes, or when several smaller issues combine together in a consistent way, or to compare boys' responses with those of girls. We don't have the space to report every single quote, but we have tried to give as broad a range as possible. In this way we hope that we do justice to the

adolescent voice. All quotes from the teenagers are presented in italics, followed
by the gender of the respondent: [m] for male, and [f] for female.

Here we consider the first two of the questions relating to the influences on
young people's feelings.

Things which make me happy

We decided to ask the young people to write down 'three things which make
me happy' because, from our experience of groupwork with teenagers, young
people seem quite to enjoy creating lists and find this task relatively easy. This
also ensures that the young people don't spend too much time writing down
loads of things and miss out on the chance to complete other questions.

In Howie Feel we find that teenagers identify a wide range of factors as
making them happy. Some issues are mentioned by only a few, whilst others
are more commonly expressed.

The responses for all of the questions in the middle section (factors affecting
mood, self-value and outlets for feelings) suggest that there are three main
influences on young people's emotions: other people, what the young people
themselves do, and the situations in which they find themselves. These three
areas of influence, although somewhat broad, provide a helpful framework for
us to explore influences on young people's feelings a little more closely.

Other people

Other people and their actions commonly feature as sources of happiness:

- when people make me feel welcome and wanted [f]
- people being kind to me [f]
- people that make me laugh [f]
- people being nice to me [f]
- being around people I like [f]

These 'people' may be friends or family or others with whom young people
come into contact in day-to-day life. In fact, friendship issues are identified as
sources of happiness by 49 per cent of the young people, with various qualities
of these relationships being valued. Most commonly, our young people link
this happiness to having lots of friends, good friends, friends who they could
trust, and more specific issues such as:

- being with friends who like me [f]
- spending time with my friends [m]
- friends hearing what I have to say [m]

- ° knowing I have friends to turn to [f]

- ° talking to my best friend on the phone [f]

- ° being popular [m]

Over and above these comments, a number of the teenagers (6%) state that 'having a laugh' makes them happy. Presumably this will often be with friends.

Fifteen per cent say that boyfriends and girlfriends make them happy. It is not clear, however, whether this happiness is due to the particular qualities of their boyfriends or girlfriends or whether it is about merely *having* a relationship.

The family also figures as a significant source of happiness for 16 per cent. Many identify specific family members like 'my Mum' or 'my Gran', but many also expand on why their families make them feel happy:

- ° when my parents understand how hard school can be at times [f]

- ° My Mum is having a baby [f]

- ° playing with my niece [f]

- ° when all my family are together enjoying themselves [f]

- ° when I am out with my Dad as I only see him once a week [f]

- ° sometimes if I visit my Dad's grave [f]

- ° when I speak to my Granda on the phone [f]

- ° to know I have a family who love me [f]

- ° made to feel loved at home [f]

In addition to the 16 per cent who explicitly link their happiness to their families, a small number of teenagers talk about feeling loved. Clearly, for some, such feelings may relate to their families.

There are also issues of a quite specific nature which emerge. Some identify receiving compliments and praise as sources of happiness and quite a few talk of being happy when seeing or making others happy. This leads us on to our next section, which concerns those issues that directly relate to the *actions* of the young person themselves.

Things about me

Many responses to 'things that make me happy' relate to teenagers' own actions and behaviours. Also, many value aspects of their personality, their looks and how they are feeling about themselves.

Sport features highly throughout the Howie Feel questionnaire with 24 per cent of young people stating that physical activity makes them happy. Football is the most popular sporting activity, particularly for boys, although golf, hockey, badminton, swimming and dancing are also mentioned regularly. Although for the majority of young people taking part in sport is enough to make them happy, for another four per cent it is doing well in sport which is important, for example 'scoring a goal for my team'; 'playing well'; 'winning a match'.

Twenty per cent say that going out makes them happy: going to the cinema, town, their friends' houses, parties, discos, raves, and so on. Getting drunk (4%) and taking drugs (2%) are also cited, perhaps not only because intoxication and drug use can engender pleasant sensations but also because these pursuits tend to involve the company of others.

Eleven per cent report enjoying sedentary pursuits at home, such as playing on the computer, reading books or magazines, watching television, etc. It seems likely that many of these pastimes are solitary rather than sociable.

Doing well in school is stated to be an important source of happiness by 13 per cent of the young people. In addition to this, a few write in more general terms about feeling happy when they feel that they are achieving or doing something right or when they are 'coping' – presumably with their schoolwork.

A handful of young people also choose to reflect on aspects of their personality or personal attributes which make them happy:

- I'm a good listener [f]

- my confidence [m]

- I care about people [f]

- I'm outgoing and bubbly [f]

- I'm fit and healthy [f]

- I'm a good friend [f]

Some also talk positively of their physical appearance. Often these comments are about variable rather than stable attributes:

- when I have the right gear [m]

- when my hair looks good [f]

- if I am looking good [f]

- when I'm clean [m]

A wide range of more minor themes also emerge as making young people happy: 'making people laugh'; 'not getting caught'; 'fighting'; 'winning'; 'sleeping and long lies'.

Events / situations

By far the most popular event which young people mention as making them happy is the end of the school day or week (23%). A small number also link their happiness to having no homework.

Spectator sports appear frequently and, probably because Howie Feel Day fell on the day after a big football match in Glasgow, a lot of young people reveal their allegiances to certain football teams in their questionnaires. For those teenagers who support the team that won (or, in fact, opposed the team that lost), Howie Feel day was a happy one, with 12 per cent of young people expressing their pleasure at the result!

Small numbers mention high days and holidays – Christmas, Guy Fawkes, birthdays and going on holidays.

Other issues

Of course, 1634 young people writing down three things that make them happy will generate 4902 responses! We cannot possibly attempt to feedback every single one of these but we can report on the most common. Eleven per cent say that money makes them happy – winning the Lottery, earning, having or spending money. Less popular responses include the weather, pets and animals, presents, food, music and the future. The quotes below give an idea of the sorts of responses which are made:

- rainbows [m]
- a day when everything agrees with you [f]
- sunshine with a breeze [f]
- cats sitting on my knee purring [f]
- when the wars in Bosnia have ended [f]
- my dog's pregnant! [m]
- feeling safe [f]
- food, especially chocolate [f]
- if we have somewhere to go at night it is good [f]
- getting a surprise [m]
- Pamela Anderson's upper body [m]

Differences between what makes girls and boys happy

Throughout the entire Howie Feel questionnaire girls consistently seem to be more 'people oriented' than boys. Here, for instance, we see that there are twice as many girls than boys saying that friendships make them happy. Similarly, girls more often say that their happiness depends on their romantic relationships, their families, going out, people being nice to them, feeling loved, having a laugh, others being happy and receiving compliments. There is a sense then that girls more than boys link their happiness to a world of *people*.

On the other hand, boys are more likely than girls to say that their happiness is dependent on their own actions, particularly playing sport. The boys in Howie Feel are almost four times more likely than girls to say that participating in sport makes them happy (40% versus 10%). In addition to these comments, boys more than girls talk of the importance of doing well in sport (7% versus 2%). This could be because more boys take part in sport than girls or because they just enjoy it more.

More boys than girls talk of enjoying sedentary pursuits at home – mostly playing with the computer (15% versus 6%). Although the numbers mentioning drugs and sex are smaller, these are more male issues in Howie Feel.

One further clear gender difference cannot be overlooked. Whilst 22 per cent of boys consider that a favourable football result makes them happy, only 3 per cent of the girls say so.

Whether these differences between girls and boys are the result of socialisation processes is not for us to debate. However, the patterns of differences in 'things that make me happy', and throughout the questionnaire, are consistent and worthy of consideration.

Things that make me unhappy

We asked the young people to list 'three things which make me unhappy', and find that some of the things which young people consider to make them unhappy are the antithesis of things that make them happy (e.g. doing well in school versus not doing well in school). However, there are also a range of other issues which they identify as sources of unhappiness.

Other people

Many of the teenagers highlight the ways in which others can make them feel unhappy:

- ○ people putting pressure on me [m]
- ○ people taking my freedom away [m]
- ○ when people don't understand me [f]

Figure 3.1   *Laura Cook*

- ° people not taking me seriously [m]

- ° people calling me stupid [f]

- ° if nobody listens to me [f]

- ° when people treat me like a baby [f]

- ° not being appreciated [f]

- ° the way people look at you because the way you are dressed smartly going to school [f]

- ° people killing animals [m]

- ° jealous people and posers [f]

A significant number of others link their unhappiness to getting blamed unfairly, getting into trouble, being told what to do, not getting their own way, seeing others unhappy, and seeing or hearing others arguing.

Twenty per cent of teenagers cite difficulties in their friendships as sources of unhappiness. Typically such difficulties involve falling out, arguing or not talking to friends, and more specific problems:

- ○ when I find out that one of my friends is taking drugs [f]

- ○ always getting put down by friends and made out to be stupid [f]

- ○ my friends not caring [f]

- ○ when one of my friends starts all his shite [m]

In addition to the 20 per cent who write of their friendship difficulties, 7 per cent are unhappy about 'slagging' (being ridiculed), 9 per cent identify bullying and a small number say they feel unhappy when others talk behind their backs.

In Chapter 11 we will see that 'romantic relationships' feature significantly in Howie Feel. It is, therefore, unsurprising that teenagers also include 'getting dumped' and 'getting knockbacks' in their lists of 'things that make me unhappy'.

Unsurprisingly, teenagers also hold family members responsible for their unhappiness. Twelve per cent talk of not getting on with their parents:

- ○ arguing with my parents [f]

- ○ being nagged by my Mum and Dad [m]

- ○ my Mum and Dad annoying me [f]

- ○ when my Dad or Mum clips my ear [m]

Over and above these 12 per cent who identify not getting on with their parents, some single out their mums (2%) or their dads (2%) and issues specific to them:

- ○ my Mum feeling depressed [m]

- ○ when my Mum goes out at night alone [f]

- ○ seeing my father [m]

- ○ when my mum doesn't talk to me because it makes me feel unloved [f]

- ○ my Mum being patronising or unreasonable [f]

- ○ if my Mum takes her boyfriend's side in a argument [f]

Some teenagers give responses describing aspects of home life which, although not always directed at them, are sources of unhappiness:

- ○ my parents are getting divorced, not knowing what the future holds [f]

- ○ when my Mum and Dad are angry and they fight [f]

- ○ being at home with my Mum and brother [f]

- ○ my big sister has one rule for herself and another rule for me [f]

The final category of people making an appearance on teenagers' unhappy lists are teachers, mentioned by 5 per cent.

Things about me

We saw earlier that many teenagers say that doing well in school makes them happy. Conversely, 12 per cent cite doing badly in school as a source of unhappiness. Most commonly, such responses are about getting bad marks in tests, not coping with school work, failing to understand particular subjects, etc. Eight per cent of teenagers complain about having to get out of their beds for school in the first place.

In fact, the most frequently recurring issues arising in teenagers' lists of 'things that make me unhappy' relate to school, with 23 per cent making responses such as 'hate school', 'being at school', 'having to come to school', 'this dump', etc. In addition to this 23 per cent, some are more specific about feeling unhappy about more certain aspects of school life, such as homework – particularly when they feel the amount is excessive (14%) – tests and exams (5%), specific class subjects (5%) and getting into trouble at school (3%).

We find that a number of young people (3%) talk of feeling lonely. This includes those young people who don't feel popular, who say they don't have any friends or who say that they are unhappy being alone:

- needing to talk to somebody about a problem and being alone [f]

- not having anyone to talk to in time of need [f]

- feeling when nobody likes you [f]

We know that mental health and physical health are interrelated. In Howie Feel, 4 per cent link feeling unwell to feeling unhappy – feeling sick, sore heads and sore stomachs are the most commonly mentioned. We wonder how many of these teenagers are reporting physical symptoms of their own stress.

We will see later that the way young people feel about their own bodies can have a marked influence on their emotional health. In this part of the questionnaire a number of teenagers list either their looks in general or specific aspects of their physical appearance (clothes, face, nose, ears, spots, hair, legs and being fat) as sources of unhappiness. Others talk of feeling unhappy about various more abstract attributes:

- feeling unconfident [f]

- being uptight [f]

- I'm lazy [m]

- being drunk to have sex [f]

- ◦ feeling when everything is getting on top of you [f]
- ◦ knowing I'm going to get old [f]
- ◦ having bad feelings [m]
- ◦ when I can't get to sleep at night [f]

Events/situations

In their unhappiness list, 11 per cent identify illness and death – most commonly amongst close family members:

- ◦ my mother dying on me [m]
- ◦ people dying for no reason [m]
- ◦ someone I know getting cancer [f]

In Chapter 2 we saw that many teenagers describe themselves as 'bored' and 'fed up' in our Field of Words. Here we find that 5 per cent of the teenagers cite that having nothing to do or being bored makes them unhappy. This is, perhaps, not surprising, or the fact that being grounded (9%) and staying in (11%) are also identified. Finally, just as a large number of young people put their football team winning on their list of things that make them happy, so too do a similar proportion (11%) say they are unhappy when the team they support loses or when the team they oppose wins!

Other issues

The remaining issues that make young people unhappy are quite wide-ranging. For example, the weather (the rain, the cold and the damp) is mentioned by over 6 per cent. Less commonly, some identify being skint, violence and their fears about going out, domestic chores, racism and current affairs.

Differences in what makes girls and boys unhappy

As friendships are much more likely to be cited by girls than boys as sources of happiness, it is perhaps unsurprising that friendship difficulties also feature more prominently in the accounts of the girls than in those of the boys. Just as 'people' issues make the girls happy, they also can make them unhappy – not getting on with parents and seeing others unhappy are more commonly flagged up by girls than their male counterparts. We also see that 'being grounded' and staying in are more commonly expressed by girls, possibly because such constraints remove young people from their friends.

We saw earlier that girls are more likely than boys to describe themselves as 'unconfident'. This lack of confidence may increase anxiety in difficult

Figure 3.2 *James Fearn*

situations and may partly explain why exams are cited as a source of unhappiness by more girls (8%) than boys (3%).

Predictably, boys are much more likely than girls to write that their football team losing makes them unhappy (22% versus 2%). Similarly, boys talk more than girls about losing in general. Finally, although the numbers doing so are small, getting into trouble seems to be more of a boys' issue than a girls' one.

When we consider teenagers' responses to the first two questions of the Howie Feel survey we see a remarkable consistency – the picture we get from asking girls and boys what makes them happy is consistent with the picture we get when we ask what makes them unhappy. Furthermore, the issues here are congruent with some of those which emerge later in the questionnaire.

This chapter then has started to give us a feel for what makes young people tick. That is not to say that we can making sweeping generalisations about them – they're a diverse group. Furthermore, when we say that boys are more likely to say this and girls to say that, we do not mean to imply that boys in general say this and girls in general say that. Rather, any sex differences are a matter of *degree*. In later chapters we will continue to see evidence of gender differences, some of which are striking.

Our insight into the emotional world of young people is continued and deepened in our next chapter, which considers how young people feel about themselves.

CHAPTER 4

Self-Esteem
What Makes Young People Value Themselves

How young people feel about themselves is important. The extent to which they value themselves, that is their self-esteem, can play an important role in protecting against mental ill-health (such as depression). We return to this in later chapters.

In our survey we asked young people to write down what makes them feel good and bad about themselves, that is what affects their self-esteem. It should be noted that we did not ask *if* they feel good or bad about themselves; our questionnaire then is not designed as a diagnostic tool. Rather, we hope that the questionnaire will paint a picture of those issues impacting upon and shaping the emotional lives of young people.

This chapter considers these influences on feelings about *self*. We will start on a positive note.

Things that make me feel good about myself

We asked young people to list 'three things which make me feel good about myself'.

Feeling good about oneself is very different to feeling happy and, although there is some overlap between the two sets of responses, the young people approach the questions 'things that make me happy' and 'things that make me feel good about myself' in very different ways.

Other people

Just as other people make young people feel happy, they also can make teenagers feel good about *themselves*:

- being surrounded by nice people (esp. boys) [f]

- when lots of people speak to me [f]
- people look up to me [m]
- people like me [m]

Sixteen per cent say that their friends make them feel good about themselves. For some this is due to feeling popular ('having lots of friends'), for others it is more to do with their friends' behaviour towards them (e.g. 'my friends respect me'). A few teenagers also value having a laugh with friends.

As adolescence is a time when young people begin to fancy others, it follows that boyfriends and girlfriends have an influence on how young people feel about themselves (11%):

- when girls say they like you [m]
- girls running at my feet [m]
- getting whistled at by guys in cars [f]
- I'm going with a good looking girl [m]

Some teenagers talk of feeling loved:

- knowing I am loved [f]
- when people care about me [f]

For some, these feelings may relate to their families – certainly families do feature in 5 per cent of the teenagers' lists:

- when my Mum or Dad say I love you [f]
- that my parents trust me [f]

Thirteen per cent of the young people remind us that receiving compliments makes them feel good about themselves:

- when I am congratulated for doing well [m]
- when people say to me 'well done' [f]
- my friend saying I am strong [m]

The fact that so many teenagers value compliments emphasises the influence of positive feedback on their self-esteem.

Things about me

It may surprise us that doing well in school is the most commonly identified source of self-esteem across *all* the schools taking part in our survey. The fact that the questionnaires were carried out in the school setting may, of course, bias the responses, but the fact that 37 per cent of young people choose to write this reflects the importance teenagers place on educational achievement. Doing well is not always about being top of the class, it can also involve getting good marks, coping with the classwork and being proud of how one is doing in school:

- getting awards for good behaviour [f]
- getting better grades than other people [f]
- answering questions [m]
- when I get higher marks than my sister [m]

In addition to these achievements, 2 per cent say that finishing their homework makes them feel good about themselves.

Some young people (13%) talk in a more general way about achievements – these may or may not relate to school issues:

- doing something I don't think I can do [m]
- when I do something that makes me proud [m]
- when I make my Dad proud [m]
- knowing that I can cope with what the world throws at me [f]
- knowing I am pleasing others with my efforts [m]

As we saw in the previous chapter, a lot of young people say that physical activity makes them happy. Whilst participating in sport *in itself* is not identified as making young people feel good about themselves, 28 per cent identify winning or achieving at sports as sources of self-esteem. Teenagers value both being successful as an individual – 'being good at football (for a girl!)' – and being part of a winning team – 'the team I play for are at the top of the league'.

Many of the responses to 'things that make me feel good about myself' suggest that young people do not just gain satisfaction from doing things that directly benefit themselves. Doing things for *others* can be an affirming experience and 23 per cent talk of feeling good about themselves when they are being nice to others:

- giving people a shoulder to cry on [m]
- just really being there for somebody when they need a friendly face [f]
- when I get friends to make up [f]
- my friends are going out with someone because of me [f]
- the looks on my family's faces when they receive presents that I have saved for [f]

- ° walking an OAP's dog [m]
- ° cooking the dinner at night and giving my Mum a break [m]

A significant number of young people (9%) delineate aspects of their personality and identity in their lists of things that make them feel good about themselves. These are wide ranging:

- ° my friendliness [f]
- ° the way I can talk myself out of things [f]
- ° I am not a virgin [m]
- ° I am me [m]
- ° my liveliness, my free spirit [f]
- ° the way I come up with lots of ideas [m]
- ° I am a good liar [f]
- ° not being a spoilt child [f]
- ° I have grown up and I am a big boy and I'm nearly a man [m]
- ° knowing that I am not gay [m]
- ° knowing that I never have and never will sleep with a woman [m]
- ° I come from a high class family [f]
- ° I have started shaving [m]

Some also single out their own specific actions as making them feel good:

- ° taking the mickey out of my ma [m]
- ° being able not to eat for ages [f]
- ° earning my own money [m]
- ° feeling independent and in control of myself and my life [f]
- ° satisfying my boyfriend [f]

Eight per cent say that they feel good about themselves when they look good or when they are wearing nice clothes (11%):

- ° If I look good I feel good [f]

Other issues

A few miscellaneous issues spring up in this section of the questionnaire. We see that other 'things which make me feel good about myself' include: having money, feelings about the future, having responsibility and drinking alcohol. One boy even manages to make us feel good about ourselves by writing 'Howie Feel day'!

Differences in what makes girls and boys feel good about themselves

Girls are twice as likely as boys to say that friends (21% versus 10%) and family (7% versus 2%) affect the way they feel about themselves. Similarly, receiving compliments appear twice as often in girls' accounts (18% versus 9%).

Girls are also more likely than boys to talk of issues relating to body-image. It would seem than when girls feel good about aspects of their physical appearance, such as their looks, clothes, hair and weight, their self-esteem is affirmed, whereas the majority of boys don't seem to place such a high value on the way they look.

The self-esteem of the boys in our survey, on the other hand, seems to be affected by their own achievements. Forty-two per cent of boys compared to 8 per cent of girls say that winning and achieving at sports makes them feel good about themselves. Boys are also more likely to talk of achievements in general. Interestingly, whereas girls are more likely than boys to identify a relationship ('my boyfriend') as making them feel *happy*, boys are much more likely than girls (18% versus 7%) to identify a relationship ('my girlfriend') as making them feel *good about themselves*. This issue is picked up in Chapter 11.

Things that make me feel bad about myself

How much someone values themselves (their self-esteem) can affect how vulnerable s/he will be to the trials and tribulations of life. Those who have a low opinion of themselves may be less likely to feel they have control over their lives and may allow situations, events and people to get the better of them. In this question we look at those influences on self-esteem that may cause young people to feel *bad* about themselves.

Other people

We saw earlier that other people can make teenagers feel good about themselves, for example by giving them compliments. Here we see ways in which others make them feel bad about themselves:

- when you play absolutely awful in a hockey match and people tell you [f]
- when no-one speaks to me [f]
- when people act like I am strange [f]

- the way people treat me [f]

More specifically, 7 per cent of the teenagers identify 'being slagged' (made fun of) and being put down (5%):

- when I get called names [f]
- when people call coloured people names and when people call me a nigger lover [f]
- when people say I am fat and say I don't wear fashionable things [f]
- when someone puts me down on any of my weaknesses so I worry about them ten times more [f]
- when my teacher tells me I am worthless [m]

In addition to these complaints, 8 per cent talk of feeling bad about themselves because they do not have many friends or because they have difficulties with existing friendships. Smaller numbers also identify that they feel bad about themselves when others talk behind their backs, when they are dumped by girlfriends/boyfriends and when they are rejected:

- knowing people are talking about me [f]
- falling out with your best friend [f]
- people talking behind my back [m]

Twelve per cent of teenagers say that they feel bad about themselves when they are arguing or not getting on with their parents:

- not having a close relationship with my parents [f]
- when my Mum says she hates me and tells me to go and live with my Dad [m]
- my parents butting into my life [f]
- when Mum and Dad say how good your big sister is at school and you should be more like her and pass all your exams [f]
- Mum telling me I'm hopelessly boring [f]

Things about me

We saw earlier that doing well in school is an important source of self-esteem for many young people. *Not* doing well in school also has a large impact on their self-esteem, with 28 per cent feeling bad about themselves when they get bad marks, or when they don't understand or can't cope with their school work.

Figure 4.1   *Marie Wallace*

- when everybody does something right and I do it wrong [f]
- being last to do the questionnaire [m]
- if I don't know how to do the work and I need to ask questions all the time [f]
- I can't read [f]
- I'm not clever and I don't think I'll be able to do anything in the future [f]

Not doing well in relation to other activities also figures. In particular, not doing well in sport (6%), not winning (3%), and not doing their best (3%) all take their toll on young people's self-esteem.

Many young people also reflect on their own behaviours, particularly in the way these behaviours impact on other people. For example, 'not being good' is identified by 13 per cent of young people as making them feel bad about themselves. Typically, here teenagers talk of bullying others, stealing, cheating, not doing as they are told, truanting, starting fights, etc:

○ doing things behind my parents back [f]

○ bullying someone when I'm in a group [m]

○ putting bangers through letter boxes [m]

○ saying something I shouldn't have and putting my foot in it [m]

○ sometimes being cruel to other people (e.g. not keeping secrets) [f]

More specifically, 5 per cent talk of feeling bad about themselves when they tell lies. Also, a handful of teenagers cite drinking alcohol, smoking and swearing.

Further common behaviours that appear in teenagers' lists of 'things which make me feel bad about myself' are: not helping others (3%), hurting others' feelings (7%), slagging (ridiculing) others (4%), letting people down (4%), arguing and fighting (6%), getting into trouble (8%) and not sticking up for themselves (1%).

As well as their actions, 16 per cent write about those aspects of their personality which make them feel bad about themselves:

○ my sharp tongue [f]

○ my voice is too broad Glaswegian [f]

○ I am ruthless with money [m]

○ not being able to open up [f]

○ I get nervous and tongue-tied [gender unknown]

○ when I am shy and unconfident in a large crowd [f]

○ I am a bit daft [m]

○ I'm not outgoing enough [m]

○ sometimes I can be a bit moany [f]

Many young people (13%) identify their general physical appearance as having a negative effect on their self-esteem. In addition to these young people, there were others who singled out more specific facets of their appearance which make them feel bad about themselves:

○ the fact that I'm the smallest out of all my friends [m]

- Vogue magazine, my fat body, my hair/face [f]
- looking like a tramp [m]
- my spots
- my colour [f]
- not looking grown up [m]
- being so thin [f]
- when I don't get enough sleep and have black rings beneath my eyes [f]
- my ginger hair (sometimes) [m]
- feeling sad about not quite being up to standard in the trendy department [f]

A wide number of disparate issues also emerge which do not fit neatly into categories but are nonetheless interesting and give us a glimpse into what some young people consider to be important:

- I had to take drugs and alcohol to try and forget that I am gay [m]
- chucking my lunch out [f]
- sometimes I say things that I don't mean [f]
- knowing that people are afraid of me [m]
- if I talk to my Mum's boyfriend I feel like I am letting my Dad down [f]
- if I say NO to someone [f]
- getting my Mum all stressed up [m]
- my writing is disgraceful (as you've seen) [m]
- when I think of people who have passed away and I blame it on myself [f]
- when I can't control my temper [f]
- how I neglect my family and religion [m]
- not being able to speak to girls casually [m]
- when you misjudge someone and you say they are horrible but they actually turn out to be nice [f]
- when I wank myself [m]

- ° when I eat too much [m]
- ° having no money [m]
- ° being grounded [f]

Differences in what makes girls and boys feel bad about themselves

Once again we find clear gender differences. In response to 'things that make me feel bad about myself', girls are much more likely than their male peers to identify aspects of their physical appearance – such as their looks in general, spots and clothes. Over and above this, a staggering 10 per cent of girls mention being fat or overweight, whilst such worries are only identified by 2 per cent of the boys.

Consistent with our previous findings, girls are also more likely to cite issues which relate to other people – such as hurting someone's feelings, arguing, friendship difficulties, not getting on with parents and being put down. On the other hand, boys are far more likely than girls to feel bad about not doing well in sport (13% versus 1%) and not winning (6% versus 1%). Also, a higher number of boys than girls mention getting into trouble, fighting and not being good.

We have seen that teenagers focus on specific aspects of their personality as affecting their self-esteem. However, the nature of these attributes are *qualitatively* different between girls and boys. Whereas the most common self-critical comments which girls make are about feeling jealous, lacking confidence, being moany, moody and shy, by far the most common attribute which boys mention is their temper.

In this chapter we have looked at responses from the young people which outline the important influences on their feelings and self-esteem. Clearly there are a wide range of factors which shape the emotional health of young people. The task for us, as adults, is to work out where we fit into this picture and how we can best support young people in terms of their emotional well-being. Our next chapter gives us a clearer idea of how young people want to receive this support.

CHAPTER 5

What Young People Do With Their Feelings

Having feelings is a natural part of being human. We all experience a range of emotions – positive, negative and mixed – some of which are easier to cope with than others. So what happens when young people experience these feelings? Where do these feelings go. How are they managed? What is the best way of helping teenagers with their emotions?

In this chapter we will focus on who young people talk to about their feelings, how they cope when they feel bad and what they want others to do to support them. To do this we look at the responses to the following statements in the questionnaire:

- I can talk about my feelings to…

- If I felt bad I would…

- When I feel bad I would like it if…

I can talk about my feelings to…

Research shows that a confiding relationship can provide a buffer against depression, in women at least (Brown and Harris 1978). We presented teenagers with the unfinished sentence 'I can talk about my feelings to…' to find out if young people talk about their feelings and, if so, to whom.

Although we do not ask the teenagers to create a *list* of people they can talk to, many reveal that they do in fact talk about their feelings to more than one person. For example:

> my friends and Mum and Dad because they listen and don't make fun of me [f]

As well as identifying *specific* people whom they talk to, many give detailed reasons why they talk to certain people and not others. We feel it is important not to lose sight of these.

The vast majority (64%) say that they talk to their friends about their feelings – either friends in general or best friends:

- ° my friends because they always listen [f]

- ° one of my friends, no-one else. No-one else understands [f]

- ° only one or two of my friends (the rest will just laugh) [f]

- ° my best friend – even though she hates me! [f]

- ° my best friends and only my best friends. I cannot talk to my family [m]

- ° one of my best pals – he tells me his problems, I help him then I tell him mine and he helps me [m]

Twenty-six per cent say that they can talk to their Mums and 3 per cent say their Dads. Over and above this, 18 per cent say they talk to their parents in general (i.e. Mum *and* Dad):

- ° I sometimes talk to my Mum but I can't tell her everything or she becomes over-protective [f]

- ° my Mum and Dad. Although I am occasionally embarrassed and uneasy about confronting them. Not because they are hard to talk to – just for reasons I don't know. It's the same for everyone I suppose [m]

- ° I can talk to my Mum about some school things but I keep to myself about boys, and people going out drinking and smoking [f]

- ° My Mum – but I don't really want to [f]

As well as parents, young people also say that they can talk about their feelings to other family members such as siblings, grandparents, cousins, aunts, uncles, etc. Clearly, families can provide 'safe' environments for many teenagers to express their emotions:

- ° I can talk about my feelings to my sister, she always listens and is always there for me when I need her [f]

- ° my brother because if I have bad or evil feelings I know he won't tell my parents [m]

- ° my granny because I know she doesn't tell anybody anything [m]

Besides friends and family, young people say they talk about their feelings to their teachers (6%) and boyfriends and girlfriends (5%). A few teenagers identify certain professionals with whom they share their feelings. Only a tiny proportion say that they talk to God.

Reading the responses, we come across some teenagers who identify non-human or inanimate 'listeners':

- my 'Take That' posters [f]

- my dog – she doesn't answer back [f]

- I like writing letters or in a diary because they help to clear your thoughts [f]

- my diary…I don't trust anyone so I only keep things to myself [f]

- I just sit and talk to my Gran (but she is dead) [f]

- I also like talking to my teddy because it's as if they just listen and can't talk back [f]

Clearly, 'sounding off' to those who cannot answer back is very safe and may have its advantages! Pouring out feelings in this way may be cathartic. However, whilst such 'listeners' may be a helpful *additional* outlet for feelings for some teenagers, we wonder how many feel that they have no-one else to talk to:

> no-one as I do not have the confidence in trusting anyone. The only things I tell my feelings to are my goldfish, as they don't answer back and I let my feelings get typed out on my computer, save it and hide the file [m]

Worryingly in fact, 8 per cent assert that they have *nobody* with whom they can share their feelings:

- no-one. I don't have a best friend and my so-called friends don't care [f]

- no-one – nobody would listen to me [f]

- no-one at all, there is no point in trying anymore [f]

- nobody, no-one ever seems to understand my feelings. They think I am a kid and I have no worries – they are wrong! [f]

- I can't talk about my true feelings to anyone…(sometimes I talk to my Mum) [f]

- I don't feel I can talk to anyone. No-one seems to take me seriously a lot. I tend to bottle things up [f]

The examples above suggest that some young people feel that others don't care how they feel. For others, it is more that they *can't* or *won't* want to talk about their feelings to others:

- ○ I prefer to cover up my feelings [f]

- ○ I haven't really got the bottle to tell anyone my feelings in case they just laugh at me [m]

- ○ when I am sad I go in bad moods and don't want to talk to anyone [f]

- ○ I am not really a talk about feelings person [m]

- ○ no-one because I am too shy [m]

- ○ sometimes something is wrong and I know I just have not got the bottle to say it [m]

In the main, however, the majority of the teenagers in our survey *do* feel that they can talk to others about their feelings. If we look closely at the comments that they make, it is possible to paint a picture of the type of person that young people find it most easy to talk to. Whether they are friends or family, teachers or other professionals, these people must be trustworthy – they will not laugh or take the situation lightly; they need to be good at listening; they must be caring and sensitive to the young person's feelings; they only give advice when it is asked for. How many of us feel we truly fit this bill at all times?

Differences between girls and boys in who they talk to about their feelings

It is, of course, a stereotype to believe that *no* boys talk about their feelings, and *all* girls do. Whilst sex differences are not black and white, in Howie Feel we do see evidence of a different *pattern* of responses in girls and boys. Girls (84%) are much more likely than boys (49%) to say they talk to their friends about their feelings. They are also more likely to speak to their Mums (34% of girls versus 18% of boys).

On the other hand, boys are more likely to cite parents in general (26% versus 12%), rather than singling out one parent. Although the numbers are small, they are also more likely than girls to say that they talk to their Dads. These differences accord with research which shows that, in adolescence, mother-daughter relationships are characterised by their emotional closeness. Fathers in general have more emotionally remote relationships with their teenagers, particularly their teenage daughters (Steinberg 1987).

Although there is not much difference between the numbers of girls and boys talking to their siblings, it seems that whereas boys talk to both their brothers and sisters equally, girls tend to talk just to their sisters. Similarly, girls talk to their aunts more than their uncles, with boys talking to them equally.

Of those young people who did not talk to anyone about their feelings, they are much more likely to be boys than girls (12% versus 4%).

Of course, it is possible that boys and girls may interpret the statement 'I can talk about my feelings to…' in different *ways* – for example, in responding to this statement, do boys and girls refer to feelings of similar intensity? Susan McGinnis picks this up in Chapter 19.

If I felt bad I would…

We asked teenagers to complete the sentence 'If I felt bad I would…' to find out what young people do with any negative feelings they have; to identify their coping mechanisms.

When we look through the responses to this question, it is clear that the young people interpret it in different ways. A small number of young people respond in terms of feeling bad – as in 'I'm a bad person, evil, sinful, etc.':

- ○ tell a priest at confession [m]
- ○ if I hurt or disappointed someone, I buy them something if I have money. I'm usually more disappointed with myself [m]

We did not anticipate that young people would interpret 'bad' in this way, and perhaps we should have phrased the question in such a way that this could not have happened. However, most young people did respond in terms of feeling 'bad' as in feeling sad, worried depressed, etc.

Reading the questionnaires we see that some young people choose to find ways to release their feelings. Some try to cope with feeling bad, usually by attempting to take their minds off their worries. Others, however, seem to suppress their bad feelings by keeping things to themselves. Of course, how a young person behaves when s/he feels bad is not only dependent on individual differences between people but also the nature and available support and outlets for these feelings. It is also likely that young people will act in different ways at different times, as evidenced by the fact that many young people give more than one response to this question.

Expressing and releasing feelings…

Most commonly, teenagers say that if they felt bad they would tell someone or discuss it (38%). It would seem then that many subscribe to the belief that 'a problem shared is a problem halved':

- ○ tell someone and hope they comforted me as hopefully I would to them if they were in the same position [f]
- ○ run up the phone bill [f]

- spill out my feelings to my parents and try to feel cheerier [m]
- talk to someone and express the way that I feel [f]
- ask somebody if it was natural to feel that way about the thing I felt bad about [f]

In the main, problems are shared with mums or friends, consistent with responses in 'I can talk about my feelings to…'.

Young children can often release their feelings by crying. This way of releasing tensions and emotions continues, of course, into adolescence and beyond, and we find that in Howie Feel a number of teenagers (6%) express themselves in this way:

- cry my bad feeling away and talk to myself [f]
- sit and listen to slow songs and cry [f]
- shout and bawl in silence inside of me…sit in a dark corner and let all my feelings out through crying [m]
- at bed-time just cry and hope my parents won't notice [f]

More dramatically, perhaps, 4 per cent of young people write of violent expressions of emotions. Sometimes this violence is directed at others, as in 'hitting someone'. At other times the responses are generalised to objects or themselves:

- punch the wall [m]
- let all the pain and anger out on my bed [m]
- walk around and slam doors [f]
- take a maddy and smash things up [m]
- either hit or annoy someone because this is the only way I can feel free – not good, but as though the worries are out of my system [f]

Quite a few young people say that they would be moody or irritable and would take things out on others:

- act in a snappy way, act like an angry old fart, and also degrade people and have racist feelings [m]
- get angry and sulk [f]
- most likely take it out on my family which makes me feel worse [f]
- go in a mood and always moan at people [f]

A small number of girls find solace in their diaries and say that if they felt bad they would write down their feelings:

- ° write in my diary as it is private and no-one knows I keep it [f]

Coping with feelings

Some young people seem to cope with their feelings by trying to sort things through, working out what the problem is and attempting to find a solution. Often this happens in their own room or a quiet corner:

- ° find some place quiet where I would be alone to think [m]
- ° concentrate and think and see how I felt bad in the first place and I would sort it all out [f]

One of the most prominent coping mechanisms for our teenagers seems to involve attempts to cheer themselves up:

- ° go out and enjoy myself with my friends to have a laugh [f]
- ° go in a hot bath for a long time [f]
- ° act normally as it makes me happy [f]
- ° try and do something good and fulfil myself with life and try to think of why life is worth living [m]
- ° look on the bright side if there is a bright side [f]
- ° go out on my bike and ride for hours [m]
- ° go into my room alone, listen to music, read a magazine and eat as much junk food as I could especially chocolate [f]

This last quotation exemplifies common strategies our young people adopt to cheer themselves up – listening to music (4%), reading (1%), eating in general (3%) and eating chocolate (2%). So, overall 5 per cent talk of eating as a source of comfort:

- ° eat chocolate and go shopping with a few mates [f]
- ° try and cheer up and have a feast of food. This always cheers me up [gender unknown]
- ° stay in my house, watch TV in bed and eat loads of things that are bad for me [f]

Other situations which take the young people's minds off their problems are: going out (7%), getting drunk (2%) and others cheering them up (2%).

Keeping feelings to myself...

A number of young people attempt to manage their feelings by keeping them to themselves. Seven per cent of the teenagers in our survey write that when they feel bad they bottle up their feelings and/or do not tell anyone:

- ○ keep quiet about it [m]
- ○ try to cover it up so nobody would find out [m]
- ○ bottle it up and do stupid things like get drunk or take jellies [m]
- ○ bottle it up and hope it passes [f]
- ○ try to not let anyone know how I feel and then get depressed on my own [m]
- ○ not tell anyone because I would not like to burden anyone with my problems [f]

Over and above the 7 per cent who say that they would keep a lid on their feelings, a few young people specifically say that they would want to be left alone (2%). Unlike the teenagers who seem to want to sort out their problems, some seem less willing to take control of their situation:

- ○ like to crawl under a rock and never come out [f]
- ○ go to sleep and hope when I wake up its not there [m]

Worryingly, 3.5 per cent of the young people say they would kill themselves if they felt bad. Whether or not these reflect genuine suicide intentions, it is alarming that so many regard suicide as a solution. Whereas boys respond to the question with the blunt response of 'I'd kill myself', girls expand:

- ○ well the other night I got so upset I was going to kill myself [f]
- ○ I think if I felt bad I would get steamin' and walk out in the middle of the road, just lying there waiting for a car coming round the corner and the car would stop on time [f]
- ○ when my Mum and Dad start fighting I feel like killing myself [f]

Differences between what girls and boys do if they are feeling bad

Once again we find there are a number of differences between responses from girls and boys to this question. Girls are twice as likely than boys to share their feelings with others through telling someone or discussing their problems (50% of girls compared to 24% of boys).

Girls are more likely to cope with their bad feelings by getting others to cheer them up, listening to music and crying. Whereas only one boy talks of eating chocolate, 3.5 per cent of girls do – those who market chocolate should take note!

On the other hand, boys talk of expressing or releasing their feelings in violent ways (7%) as compared with only 1 per cent of girls. We find that boys are five times more likely than girls to say they would kill themselves (5% versus 1%). Perhaps this pattern links with the fact that there is a higher suicide rate amongst young men.

Of those young people who prefer to be left alone, more frequently these are boys. Getting drunk is a male thing more than a female thing, although the numbers are surprisingly low for both sexes.

When I feel bad I would like it if…

When we read the responses it is clear that many young people want others to get involved in helping them with their feelings. Most of the young people want to be able to express their feelings and have them heard and understood. Some want to be cheered up, while others say that they want to be left alone. What is striking though is the fact that young peoples' needs and preferences are diverse.

Talking about feelings and being listened to…

Just as many young people state that they would tell someone or discuss it if they were feeling bad – this is echoed in responses to this question – with many saying that they would like someone to talk to, usually friends or family:

- ° I could tell my friends and trust them not to say anything [f]
- ° I talked to someone who I didn't see constantly [f]
- ° I wish I could talk to my Dad a little more than I can [f]
- ° people would just shut up and let you speak out your thoughts and feelings [m]
- ° I could talk to my Mum about my problems but she doesn't listen to me and I get too embarrassed to talk to her [f]
- ° I could talk to someone in my own time [f]
- ° someone would talk to me quietly instead of yelling [m]

A small number of young people state that they would like to speak to a professional about feeling bad:

> I'm always helping other people about how they feel, no-one cares about how I feel. People always tell me their problems, I've got no-one to tell about mine…I would really like it if there was a school counsellor [m]

There was a special helpline just for teenagers where you wouldn't have to be ashamed to ask for advice – it should not be a free call because too many people just pretend they have a problem to get a laugh out of hearing your suggestions [f]

Some teenagers' responses suggest that if they felt bad they would like someone to *help* them. Such help may involve advice, reassurance or practical action:

○ someone would just come along and make it all better [m]

○ my friends helped me – because I can speak the way I want to them [f]

○ I would want my Mum to help me because she would feel good about it, because she has not really talked to me or helped me the way I want her to before [f]

○ My mum and Dad could help me as I need them to help me through my life as a teenager [m]

○ there were someone to reassure me that I was doing things right and give me confidence in myself [m]

○ somebody (i.e. my parents) to help and guide me through the difficult stages but let me make all the decisions [f]

○ someone was always there and not say they are too busy [f]

Ten per cent say they would like it if parents listened and 12 per cent say they would like their friends to do so. This suggests to us that young people may not always feel that they are being heard:

○ my mum would listen to me more carefully instead of just butting in and giving me a lecture [m]

○ somebody listened to me and tried to give me the best advice as they could…just if somebody listened [f]

○ everyone would hear how I feel [m]

○ like someone to listen to my feelings and to care for me [m]

Even when young people are heard, are they always understood? Six per cent of teenagers state they would like others to *empathise* with their feelings:

○ someone understood how I felt without me having to argue my case or people thinking I'm just being stupid or lying to them [m]

- ° people would understand and not everyone would want a proper explanation as to how I feel the way I do [f]

- ° sometimes my mother knew me properly and understood what I was like. We've grown apart and I wish we hadn't! [f]

- ° people to understand how I feel and not what they feel [f]

- ° someone came and gave me a big hug and told me they loved me. Just so long as they didn't say they understand me. Because when people think they do, they usually are wrong [f]

- ° people talked to me and understood me instead of pretending they understood [m]

In some accounts there is a sense that young people's feelings are dismissed or trivialised:

- ° my mum would help me to sort my feelings out instead of just laughing at me and telling me not to be silly [f]

- ° I could trust people not to laugh at me or look upon my problems as being insignificant [f]

Coping by being comforted or cheered up...

Very often what young people seem to want is for others to cheer them up (15%) or to be cheered up in general. There are a variety of ways in which they feel this can happen:

- ° my best friend came round to my house with a video and sweets and we would watch it together and have a gossip afterwards [f]

- ° somebody would say something nice about me even if it is a load of crap [m]

- ° I could be cheered up again with some good rave music [m]

- ° my best friend would be sympathetic but try to cheer me up instead of being sorry and not knowing what to say [f]

- ° I met a crazy millionaire who gave me all his money [m]

- ° I would want the boy I fancy to throw stones at my window and save me from unhappiness [f]

- ° if the girl I fancied said yes I would be on top of the world [m]

- ° Cindy Crawford came round my house and kissed me better [m]

- ° the school got blown up [m]

Some also talk of wanting to be comforted or reassured:

- ○ my friends told me I was cool and comforted me [m]

- ○ everybody comforted me, but didn't over do it! [f]

- ○ my Dad came home and said he'd always be there for me [f]

- ○ someone in my family told me that it's alright and it wasn't my fault – that makes the pressure go right away [m]

Wanting to be left alone to work things out...

Clearly, not all young people can or want to discuss their feelings. Ten per cent say that they wish to be left alone, without others interfering:

- ○ I would not like anybody to help me because I like to do things my own way [f]

- ○ people wouldn't interfere and make it worse [f]

- ○ some people would stay out of my way [m]

- ○ other people kept their noses out of my business [m]

- ○ I would want to deal with it myself, or be left alone [m]

- ○ everyone would stop saying what's up? [f]

Although many teenagers say they want to be left alone, we have to be careful how we interpret this. Whilst they may feel that they do not want to talk, this does not necessarily mean they want to be isolated.

Differences between what boys and girls would like to happen when they feel bad

Girls continue to show themselves to be more people-oriented than boys. They are approximately twice as likely as boys to express their wish for people (i.e. parents and friends) to listen to them. They are also twice as likely to want people to cheer them up compared to the boys. Furthermore, wanting others to know what is wrong, without having to tell them, is more of a girls' thing than a boys' one (6% versus less than 1%).

Boys are twice as likely as girls to want other people to leave them alone (14% versus 7%) and this is consistent across the other questions, where boys seem more likely to be loners than girls.

In this chapter we have glimpsed into what young people do with their feelings. Clearly many young people seek solace from others, but there are conditions to this – even once young people feel that they can trust someone with their feelings enough to open up, they have to feel that they are truly being heard, and are being taken seriously and accepted.

Not all young people have the same emotional needs, and neither do they all have the same ways of managing these needs. Some young people want to be cheered up whilst others want to be left alone. Girls and boys also have differing perspectives on ways to cope with feelings.

If we as adults want to support young people in ways which they consider to be appropriate and acceptable, we must be sensitive to, and accommodate, the very needs which stamp them out as unique individuals. How we can play our part in supporting young people is picked up in subsequent chapters by practitioners in the field of adolescence.

CHAPTER 6

Dear Diary
How We Feel

All anyone talks about is how bad teenagers today are. Well things are harder now! [f]

When we came up with the idea of Howie Feel we hoped that we would obtain a view of teenagers which reflects the range of emotions which they are experiencing in their everyday lives. For this reason we were careful not to impose any preconceived notions of adolescence on them. Therefore, we devised the questionnaire to allow the teenagers to express their feelings not only in their own words but also *on their own terms*. Nowhere was this free licence greater than in the 'Dear Diary' section. We wanted teenagers to write about whatever is important for them, to decide for themselves what they want to say about the way they feel, so we gave them a blank page headed *Dear Diary*. However, as we sat on the floor of our office tearing open 1634 envelopes, we found that we were unprepared for what we were going to read. We had wanted to glimpse into the emotional world of adolescence, yet maybe we had not expected our teenagers to so fully engage with the task of describing themselves so intimately.

Sometimes it is not so much what the teenagers say but *how* they say it. Often the accounts simply reflect the ups and downs of everyday life. Nonetheless, when we read the diaries we cannot fail to be moved by the fact that even events which we adults may consider to be trivial can be accompanied by very strong emotions in teenagers. Some of these emotions are positive, some negative and some a mixture of both. All of these feelings are real and legitimate expressions or reactions to life. To understand and support teenagers we must understand and accept the way they feel. This gets us back to our basic premise: that *how we feel matters.*

Adolescents spend a lot of their time thinking about who they are, what they are like and about their relationships, and this comes across in the 'Dear Diary' section. In later chapters we will look at what the young people write in relation to specific issues like school, family life, friends, etc. Here we focus on what teenagers say about the way they are feeling in general.

So, how are they feeling? Happy? Unhappy? Just as we would not hazard a blanket description of how 30-year-olds or 40-year-olds feel, so too must we move to a more sophisticated understanding of teenagers which considers them as a group of individuals with a wide range of experiences and feelings.

We will first look at accounts of a positive nature and then move to looking at ones which are negative. However, as the accounts of many teenagers straddle both categories, and contain both positive and negative emotions, we have included a middle section rather unimaginatively entitled *Something in Between*. Whereas subsequent chapters reveal the sorts of issues which young people describe in the 'Dear Diary' section and how these seem to impact on their feelings, this chapter gives a 'feel' for the wide *range* of emotions which emerge throughout this section of the questionnaire.

Many of the teenagers' accounts are multi-dimensional – by that we mean that they often talk of different situations and a variety of feelings, many of which are quite complex. It follows then that these experiences cannot be compartmentalised and totted up in a meaningful fashion. To analyse them, we sorted the young people's accounts into different hierarchical categories. In this way we were able to ensure that we obtained a picture which truly reflects the *relative* frequency with which issues emerge. In our reporting of the diary accounts we hope to convey this pattern by using qualifiers such as 'a few', 'many', etc and to represent all the issues or points which the young people make.

Positive emotions

Many teenagers talk of feeling happy:

> I am having a great day. Things could not have been better. I am feeling very energetic and lively and full of things to say. I have had a good laugh at lunch and at interval with my friends and I can't wait until the weekend. I had a good day in all my subjects and I do not have much homework to do today. HURRAY!!! [f]

> I feel energetic and happy. I feel as high as a kite. Ready to run the world ten times over within two days [m]

> Today I feel bloody great, as if the whole world was at my feet [m]

> I FEEL GREAT! WEEEEEEEEEEE! [m]

It feels fab to be me today because I have lots of mates and I know I am a nice guy [m]

Whereas the comments above are exultant, many others talk in more subdued tones of feeling happy or generally okay:

I am feeling fine today. Everyone seems to be having a laugh which is good. Not much to say except Blaaaaaaa! [f]

How I feel to be me today! Well I suppose it feels fine. I have got cool friends and I have a good family lifestyle. Soon there will be another baby in the family so I will be an Aunt. I am doing well at school. I play an instrument which I enjoy playing because I like music. The only thing that bothers me is my big brother's taste in music. His idea of music is the Eurovision or classical music. I mean get a life. Sometimes I am bored since I usually do the same thing every day. Bye [f]

How it feels to be me today is good because I've got a good day at school and I've got my best club after school playing football and badminton. So I am feeling excited about today. Wednesday is a good day for watching the TV as well. That's how it feels to be me today [m]

Today I feel happy, in fact I feel hyperactive. I feel as if everything is going my way. When I am happy I like it if other people are happy with me and if they talk to me [f]

I am happy with my life today because I have built up a lot of confidence in myself (except when I do English talks because I get embarrassed). I am happy because I have a brilliant best friend. I wish I had a boyfriend (who knows). My other one dumped me a few months ago. There's this guy, well three, who want to go out with me. Maybe I'll settle for one of them!! Anyway I enjoy life because I have lots of nice friends and people always compliment me on my looks!! I am glad I don't get bullied, I did in 1st Year but I told them (or him) to F*** off!! and he did!! [f]

Not all teenagers can give reasons for feeling good:

Today I feel happy about myself. I feel energetic and lively, just don't ask me why because I don't know myself [f]

It feels good to be me today. There is not some reason why I feel really happy. I love smiling and laughing so I do it all the time for no apparent reason. Laughing makes me feel good. Mum is sick and tired of hearing me laugh. She says I have to be more serious and it really annoys her. I feel as though laughing is what I need more than anything else, so I'm going to keep laughing [f]

Some of the teenagers talk of feeling resilient, with minor difficulties washing over them like water off a duck's back:

> Today I am quite happy. I have had quite a good day so far. The boy I fancy is not talking to me but I refuse to get worked up or depressed. I won't let it bother me. When I left for school this morning the bus drove straight past me but I don't really care. I guess I am just very laid back. My friend had a problem and I helped sort it out. I keep on slagging this boy about shaving his legs. It's a joke but he takes it serious. It's a shame. I even had a fight with a boy in my class. He called me a stupid cow so I battered him. When I think of what I have done today I shouldn't be happy but I am. See ya. Wouldn't want to be ya! Bye! [f]

> Today I am on top of the world. Not even my annoying brother can make me sad. I know today will be a good one even if I get into trouble from all of the teachers because today I'm going to be happy all day if I can [f]

Some seem to feel pleased with themselves:

> I feel happy. I have not got into trouble or argued with anybody. I feel proud [m]

A few teenagers speak of feeling loved and supported:

> I feel really laid back today. So far my mornings have been good. I am looking forward to today. These past few weeks have felt like this. My boyfriend is there for me. So are my friends and family. I feel like I don't have a care in the world except the ones I love and care for. Bye [f]

> I feel great, happy and I also feel wanted [gender unknown]

Some highlight their ability to cope:

> Today I am feeling happy. I am feeling the best I have felt in two weeks after the loss of a close friend. I am learning to cope with him not being there [f]

> I feel good. I'm on the top of the world. I've got plenty of friends. Life is a breeze. I'm a little worried about school but I'll cope. See you tomorrow [m]

A few teenagers say that they feel optimistic about the future, although this sentiment is more commonly expressed by boys:

> Not much going on but the chance to fulfill my ambition draws nearer every day – only four years left until I go to university and hopefully

from there I will be a fierce politician. I have extremely right-wing views. I just wish the days at university would come quickly [m]

I am feeling a bit depressed just now but I am looking forward to the future because I have made plans. I am really looking forward for school finishing and I am looking forward to getting a good job but first of all going to college and university [f]

Reading the accounts, we find that boys talk more than girls about the 'future' and what it has in store for them.

Something in between

So far in this chapter the teenagers have talked of experiencing positive emotions. However, when we *see* teenagers as happy does this necessarily reflect the way they *feel?* We come across many examples of girls wearing 'masks' which conceal their true feelings:

I feel worthless sometimes and feel unsure about my future… I put on an act that I am fine and cheerful but deep down I am confused and upset about different things [f]

I seem a happy person to my friends and joke around but I am sad inside [f]

People think I am always happy but if they see me looking sad they start annoying me. It's like I have to put on a happy face every time I am with someone [f]

I have been pretending I am happy when I am not. I am ugly, my hair is horrible, so are my clothes. So you don't want to know how I feel OK [f]

There can be a number of underlying reasons for disguising or hiding feelings, for example adhering to social norms, concealing feelings of guilt or shame, or trying to please others. This ability to cover up feelings is evident even in very young children (Hill, Laybourn and Borland 1996a).

We all have our ups and downs. However, research has shown that adolescents are particularly prone to *frequent* shifts in mood (Csikszentmihalyi and Larson 1984) and this is apparent in the 'Dear Diary' accounts:

Today I do not know how I feel. I change every five minutes [f]

This morning I didn't want to get up and go to school but when I got to school I felt better when I seen my friends. My mood changes a lot. One minute I'm chirpy, the next I'm fed up, moody and angry [m]

I am feeling a bit on the down side but it depends who I am around [m]

Today I am in a funny mood. One minute I am happy and the next I am sad. There is a disco in a few days – should I go? When it comes to girls I get all shy. I am a bit depressed about my schoolwork today. I need to work harder. If I don't I might not get a job. I feel that I have to wake up to myself. On the other hand I am quite happy. Life is too short to live. I am happy with what I have got. I have a great home and a great family. The one thing which annoys me is that I've never entered a relationship with a girl. It feels like a great weight over my shoulders [m]

It seems then that some teenagers are riding an emotional roller-coaster. This roller-coaster seems to have not only many twists and turns but rises to giddy heights and plummets into deep troughs:

Today in the morning I felt quite good because I nipped [*kissed*] the boy I fancied last night, but I don't feel good anymore 'cause my face is out in giant blotches 'cause of the bad weather and I have very sensitive skin. I really hate myself 'cause I'm fat and ugly. I feel like killing myself 'cause I hate myself so much no-one loves me [f]

In some of the accounts we see the juxtaposition of positive and negative emotions, and in some instances apparently contradictory emotions appear side-by-side:

I feel quite depressed but happy today, I can't explain it [f]

I feel bored and on top of the world [m]

I feel fine but wish I was dead because people do not like me and all think I am poor so if I felt very, very bad I would jump out of my window. I hate my life and wish it was better today [m]

In the same way as in the Field of Words (in Chapter 2), we see then that young people's feelings are not polarised but can span a spectrum of emotions, positive through to negative. This is the case for adults too (Pavis, Masters and Cunningham-Burley 1996).

The accounts so far are given by teenagers who are able to label their feelings. However, the very abstract and complex nature of feelings can make them difficult to describe and we come across some teenagers who struggle to understand why they feel the way they do:

I don't know how I feel [f]

I feel very lonely and bored but I don't know why and I feel angry but that's just me and I feel confused and I don't know why [f]

I feel loved by my parents and family. I also feel confused but I don't know why. I love my family very much. School is fine but I feel as though there is a ton on my shoulders but I am coping fine. I love all my subjects but I feel as though I am hopeless at them, but I also feel successful as well. I am so confused, especially about my feelings [f]

Today I feel confused and don't have a clear head about what I'm doing in the world. I feel as if I need some time to sort everything out like my clothes, money and friendships. I feel very tired also because I do my paper round and have to get up at 6.00 a.m. every morning and after this I have got school. So overall I feel very tired and unclear [m]

Negative emotions

Earlier we likened the Howie Feel survey to a tapestry which pulls together the accounts of all those who contributed. To build up this full picture we now move away from the colour and vitality of the positive emotions and add the darker negative feelings:

Yesterday was terrible but today I'm quiet but I'm not depressed. I'm a bit fed up with myself actually. I wish I could step into someone else for an hour [f]

I feel today down-faced and want to go home and cry in my bed. I feel like this because I want to be alone [f]

Today I am feeling very scared as you don't know what is going to happen to you in the future. Plus I feel unconfident as I am very shy and can't speak or shout like everyone else. I feel jealous of some people that walk around with better stuff. So you could say at the moment I'm depressed and fed up [f]

I feel very tired today. I don't know what's wrong with me. I can't face another day at school. I need to sort out things like friendships and the like. Overall I feel terrible [m]

Life's crap. Nothing to do that hasn't been done already. Not allowed legally to do anything until 16 then 18. So we do whatever under age and then get into trouble for it – there's nothing else to do. You can just have stay-overs, but there's nothing exciting to do apart from get drunk and play with fireworks and shoot air guns at things, which we just get into trouble for, and then we're stopped from having stay-overs so we do something else, somewhere else. What can we do? LIFE'S CRAP [m]

Many teenagers talk of a whole constellation of issues combining to make them feel low. Whilst individual issues may be manageable, the cumulative impact of various stresses *in combination* can feel overwhelming:

I feel incredibly thick and stupid. I feel angry because everybody seems to be against me and people are always teasing me. I feel jealous – everybody else's life seems so perfect. Teachers don't understand me. I don't think anybody does. All anybody does is talk about how bad teenagers today are. Well things are harder now! [f]

I wish I wasn't me. I feel fat and ugly. No boys are ever interested in me. My schoolwork isn't very good. I hate school. Girls in my class are so bitchy towards me. I feel ashamed of the way I look. I wish my Gran and Grandpa were alive. I miss them so much [f]

Some people are pissing me off. They ignore me one minute, then are really friendly the next. I wish I had one really best friend I could confide in. I wish I was slim and pretty. I would really like a boyfriend but none of the boys like me enough to go out with me. My day has been OK but my life is pretty crap. It is pretty boring. I have no social life. Sometimes I wish I was dead [f]

Perhaps few parents will be surprised about the frequency with which teenagers write of feelings of boredom. For some it is the monotony and incessant routine of daily life which gets to them, for others it is the lack of excitement or stimulation:

Today I feel bored. My life is just the same day after day. I want something exciting to happen [f]

Today was exactly like last Thursday and the Thursday before that. It feels like I am just going through the motions, doing exactly the same thing time and time again. Sometimes I just want to break out and do something totally different but I know if I did my world would turn upside down [f]

Today like usual I got up at 6.38 a.m., got dressed, took my dog out, went to school. BORING. I am very tired [m]

I feel bored and fed up because I am in school in English. I am day-dreaming about something. I am so fed up and bored I do not know what I am day-dreaming about [gender unknown]

I've felt bored and frustrated since I got up… Things always go slow for me and I don't have anything in my power to stop them [f]

Time and time again, teenagers talk of feeling tired:

I feel very tired today and I feel as if someone has hit me over the head with a heavy mallet [m]

Today I feel confused. That's only because I'm tired and I always have so much to do. I have homework. I have guitar lessons, Tae Kwan Do and backstage with the school. These are all out of school time though which means I get practically no spare time to get myself back to normal. I have to practice as much as possible and I also do piano theory which means it's all squashed in. The thing is I need free time, I need to relax… It's a hard life indeed for me and I'm starting to hate it [f]

When I got up this morning I was really tired and just felt like I couldn't handle school today. I've been like that all week. I just feel so worn out that I can't be bothered doing anything [f]

As adults nowadays we talk so much about feeling stressed. However, in Howie Feel we see that we do not have a monopoly on these feelings:

I feel tired and stressful and not coping very well just now. Today I have had a bad day and feel moody. I shout at people because I'm getting a wee bit moany. I feel scared at night and can't get to sleep. I have sore heads thinking of things happening in my life. I have had a really bad day [f]

I am stressed because I almost killed someone with a firework. Please forgive me God [m]

Sometimes I feel stressed out and when people come close to me I want to punch them. I only feel stressed when I have a lot of homework to do or the family are arguing. I get annoyed quite easily [m]

Several talk of feeling lonely, lacking emotional support:

Today I feel unwanted [m]

I feel lonely and trapped because I have no-one to talk to [m]

Today I feel very uncomfortable and unhappy. I feel on a different level from everyone else. I feel sore as I can't see my mum or brothers until I am 16 [m]

Of course, having people around does not itself guarantee that a person will receive emotional support. Furthermore, lack of support from some people may be offset by support from others:

I feel lost and on my own. The only individual I can seek comfort from is my girlfriend. She is beautiful, kind and caring [m]

Some teenagers talk of experiencing anger:

I am feeling depressed, angry at being called fat, it really gets me down when this happens but my friend helps me [f]

Happily, the girl above was able to be supported in her (very understandable) anger. However, both in the 'Dear Diary' accounts as well as elsewhere in the questionnaire we see less evidence of boys sharing these sorts of feelings with others:

> I hate it when I get angry at the smallest thing and keep it to myself, and I hate the fact that one day I am going to have to let it all out [m]

> I am very depressed today because I am not getting on well with others and I am angry because nobody cares about me [m]

Many of the teenagers experiencing distress describe themselves as depressed. Whilst some of these accounts set off alarm bells for us, clearly we cannot delineate between those who actually are clinically depressed and those who are using the term loosely. Notwithstanding, we cannot ignore the very real distress that these young people are experiencing:

> Today I am very depressed like I am most days. I am in a dump called XXXXX [children's home]. My mum isn't speaking to me because I keep running away. Also the staff won't let any of my friends phone me or let me phone them. The only good thing about today is that I am still allowed to go to mainstream school. I am very tired 'cause the staff wake me at 6.15 a.m. to go to school. I wish I was dead. I have no-one I can speak to. People keep saying that they are concerned for me but no-one is doing anything to get me out of the assessment centre. I've already slashed my wrists, it didn't work, I'm still alive. I wish I wasn't. I wish I was still staying in my children's home near my family and friends. I would be good. No-one believes that I have learned from my mistakes and I would behave. I have not had a drink for a long time but I feel that it's the only thing I can turn to [f]

> I've been depressed for a few days because I'm so fat and ugly and I want a boyfriend. I am just so depressed. I need a life [f]

> My life is depressing, I'm bored, there's nothing to do...HELP US TEENAGERS [f]

> Well recently I was at the doctor's with depression and I was so uptight...I wish I could move away and never come back because I hate my school and home and where I live [f]

> Today has been like usual – depressing. I feel like my life is a total waste of sperm [f]

Some of those who say they feel depressed cannot identify why they feel so low:

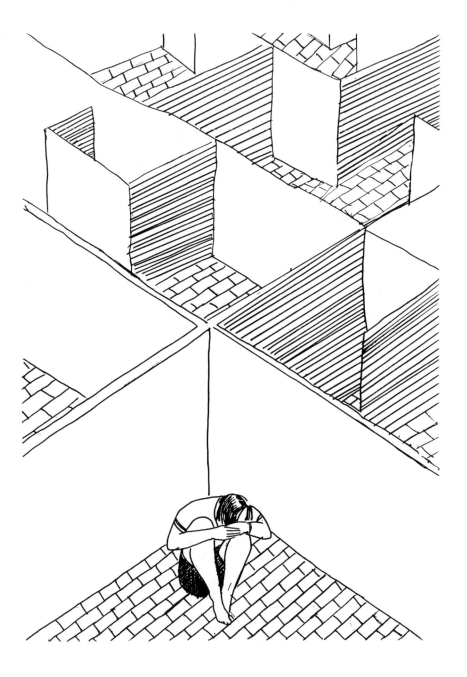

Figure 6.1   *Laura Sime*

For the past week or so I have been feeling very depressed. I don't know why. I haven't got my reasons [f]

Today I feel quite tired although I went to bed early last night. My tummy feels quite tight most of the time, all day today. I feel quite depressed lately. I don't know quite why I feel like this [f]

For others the feelings of depression have a more obvious source, such as bereavement or worries about the future:

Today I am feeling altogether rubbish. I feel like the world has no meaning. I am starting to doubt that there is a God. I wish I could tell someone but it's just too hard to explain. [Following bereavement] I felt so alone with feelings, feelings I have never had before. Every night I lie awake thinking if there is a God, why did he let this happen. I feel there is no time to grieve because XXXX is so upset and has turned to me for support. When I went to the church service I found myself so lost, lost in all my emotions for XXXX (bereaved). But I did not cry. This does not make me feel any better, not being able to let out how I feel and cry [f]

I feel depressed because I want to have a good job and a good future to support my family. I am scared in case I won't get a good job [m]

(I am) feeling sad that I'm not happy with my life. I don't know how to deal with the way I feel and I don't even know why I feel this way. You could say I was depressed. I think my life will never get better and that makes me even more sadder. I want to get out of this life. I hate it! [f]

Distressingly, some teenagers talk of suicide as a solution to their depressed feelings:

This morning I just wanted to stay in my bed and block everyone and everything out. None of my friends live near me... I'd probably kill myself if I had the guts but instead I just go out and get drunk. It's the best solution. Nobody understands me [f]

I feel depressed and unliked. Sometimes I feel suicidal. It is on a rare occasion when I smile. Only when I take stuff [m]

Depressed again. I was depressed last night and thought about killing myself. I think I might. Nobody cares anymore. They think I am a dead loser anyway. They think I am a dead loss or something. I am going away next week, me and my pal for ever. We're not coming back, there's no point. I've been thinking about my children's panel and I've to get therapy. That scares me a bit, I don't want to see a psychiatrist. A teacher said something today that really hurt my feelings, so my feelings are hurt and depressed [f]

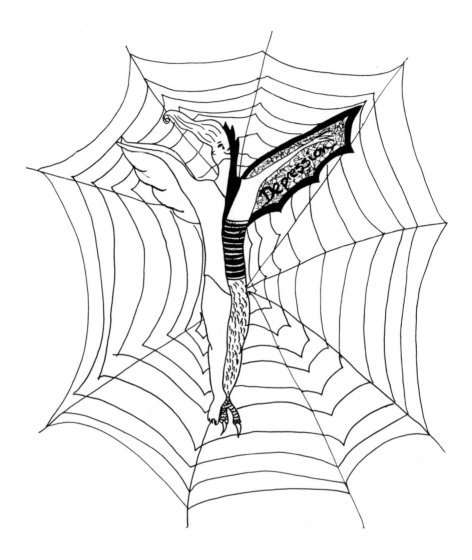

Figure 6.2   *Brienne Burgess*

I hate school. I hate my life. I've thought about killing myself but I always chicken out. My life is not worth living. I want a boyfriend but no-one wants me. The only way I can escape is by listening to music – The Doors, The Small Faces and The Beatles. I wish I was born 40 years ago in the 60s. I want to meet Jim Morrison but no chance so I might as well face the truth. I'm stuck in this well for years. I can't cope at school and no-one understands me. Why do we live? [f]

These accounts speak for themselves in terms of reflecting the levels of distress which some teenagers are experiencing. When we combine these desperate expressions with other accounts which suggest depressive feelings we cannot fail to be moved by the difficulties experienced by a significant proportion of young people. Clearly, the adolescent years are a difficult time for many.

In considering the mental health of distressed young people we must recognise that the risk of problems (such as depression) is closely linked to an individual's *perception* of his or her problems and his or her *perceived* ability to cope. In Chapter 16 Sally Butler discusses how we can promote resilience in young people, thereby reducing their chances of becoming overwhelmed by negative feelings such as those which we have seen in this chapter.

CHAPTER 7

How We Feel About Ourselves

Who am I? To answer this we must consider the *way* we see ourselves (our self-image) and the extent to which we *value* ourselves (our self-esteem) as these will shape our understanding of who we are – our identity.

Answering the question 'who am I?' is difficult for adolescents for a variety of reasons: first, adolescents find themselves inside a body which is undergoing considerable changes both in size and shape – the inevitable consequences of the passage through puberty. In order to describe themselves, teenagers must, therefore, develop a sense of 'me' which incorporates this changing physical self. Second, adolescents' thinking changes dramatically from childhood thinking and is much more reflective and abstract. Whereas a child may describe herself as 'a blue-eyed girl and owner of a hamster called Elvis', teenagers have the capacity to think in a deeper way about their beliefs, feelings, etc – to contemplate their navel, so to speak. Since the answer to 'who am I?' will be based on these more abstract thoughts for the teenager, this may lead to a distorted description of oneself. For example, one of the girls in our survey calls herself 'a fat repulsive bitch'. The observation that she is fat may or may not be true, and the 'repulsive' and 'bitch' are obviously concepts which have been linked to how she feels about 'fatness'.

Who am I? It depends… As teenagers move from childhood to adulthood they adopt changing roles and relationships. Furthermore, they may behave in different ways with different people. One of the boys in our survey sums this up when he says: 'If I'm around some girls I tend to be shy, but if I'm with my pals, I'm loud and proud'. Many parents will testify to the fact that whilst their teenager may be withdrawn with them, they may be the life and soul of the party with their pals. 'Who I am' can therefore depend on 'who I am *with*'. This presents the teenager with the dilemma of developing an integrated view of herself/himself which pulls together all these views of self.

What is our view of adolescents? Sometimes we treat teenagers as kids and sometimes we expect them to behave as adults. No clear cut-off point divides childhood from adolescence or adolescence from adulthood. Because adolescence is ambiguously defined, our expectations and behaviour towards teenagers are likely to be variable too, and this will have a knock-on effect as to the way they see themselves.

The picture we *all* have of ourselves influences not only the way we *behave* but also the extent to which we *value* ourselves (our self-esteem). In the Howie Feel accounts many of the teenagers give us a glimpse of how they see themselves, and how much or how little they value themselves.

Positive feelings about self

In 'Dear Diary' we find that boys make more positive comments about themselves than the girls do. (This is consistent with our earlier finding that boys are more likely than girls to circle the item 'pleased with myself' in the Field of Words on the first page of the questionnaire.)

So, what kind of positive comments about themselves do the young people make?

> I'm at total peace with myself today. I don't care what anyone says. I'm on a natural high. Life is good and so am I [m]

> I feel happy, confident and generally good about myself [m]

> I am pleased to be me and I am happy with who I am [f]

Whereas some of the teenagers talk of how they feel about themselves *overall*, for most these value judgements are restricted to a particular feature or aspect of their lives. For instance, physical appearance is by far the most common feature which the girls talk about, although for only a handful are these feelings of a positive nature:

> I feel good about my figure apart from the flab I have [f]

> I feel comfy in what I am wearing. That also makes me feel confident [f]

We should be careful not to dismiss feelings about appearance as shallow or superficial. There is a large body of research which reveals that the effects of personal appearance are far reaching. Not only are physically attractive people often perceived to possess more desirable personal attributes, they are also better *liked* than those who are regarded as physically unattractive. It seems then that the way teenagers look may influence the ways in which others view and relate to them. Clearly the attitudes and behaviour displayed by others can then impact on how young people see and value *themselves*.

In the 'Dear Diary' accounts we do not find many more instances of teenagers viewing themselves in positive ways. Those which remain do, however, fall fairly neatly into four categories, which have been identified by other research as shaping the way we feel about ourselves (Coopersmith 1967; Epstein 1973; Harter 1983). These categories are: feeling accepted by others, feelings about achieving and achievements, feeling in control and 'virtue' – that is 'being good'

So, first we see that being socially accepted seems to make some feel better about themselves:

> It feels fab to be me today because I have lots of mates and I know I am a nice guy [m]

> I am trying to gain confidence with people around me and I think that I am being quite successful however I do not want to show off and be too confident [m]

Next we see that some link feeling good about themselves with their achievements either in school or in sport:

> Right now I feel good. I am good at most sports and I am fit and go to sports clubs. I also feel good about myself about what I have achieved in school because I have good marks for my tests and I am in good rated classes [m]

> I think I am quite brainy and confident...I hope I keep getting good results and hope things go my way...I feel that tomorrow and in the future I will be a better person [m]

> I am fairly happy about myself and have been working hard to achieve my goals [f]

Others make comments which seem to reflect their sense of being in control of their lives or destiny:

> Today I feel happy but I am always happy. I don't let anything get me down. I feel as if I can face the world and anything it challenges me with. I don't care if anyone puts me down because I can always get up stronger than ever [f]

> Today I feel reasonably confident and want to pursue my dream of studying medicine at college [m]

The final category is that of 'virtue' – basically, 'being good'. This theme recurs more commonly amongst boys than girls:

> I feel happy. I have not got into trouble or argued with anybody. I feel proud [m]

> I feel good today because I went a whole day without stealing or getting a punny [*punishment exercise*] [m]

I feel happy today because I worked well, and behaved myself [m]

We are left with only one response which does not fall into the above classification:

Today I phoned 192 and called the woman a sweary word. Now I feel really, really, really, really bad. NOT [m]

Negative feelings about self

Some of the teenagers hold negative views of themselves which they express in quite general terms:

The way I feel is not as good as the others [m]

[*I feel*]…rubbish, failure, hopeless, stupid, angry and want to inflict pain on somebody [m]

Today I feel sad and tired. I am not happy with myself [m]

Here, and elsewhere, teenagers talk about lacking confidence:

Sometimes I don't feel confident and a lot of people say I'm shy [m]

Usually I feel unconfident in answering out/reading [m]

Reading the accounts we see marked gender differences in what seems to make boys and girls feel bad about themselves. For girls it is their appearance; one girl after another talks of feeling desolate and of little value because of the way she looks (or thinks she looks):

I am not really happy with who I am. I don't mind who I am, it's just the way I look. I often just look at others and wish I was like them [f]

Last week I felt depressed and lonely. I felt so ugly. My skin was playing up due to periods. My periods make me feel so dirty [f]

'Feeling fat' emerges as the number one issue responsible for girls failing to value themselves:

I don't have a boyfriend 'cos I am a fat repulsive bitch. The way I feel is like topping myself [f]

Sometimes I hate myself and sometimes I don't. I hate myself today because I think I'm fat and ugly [f]

I wish I wasn't me. I feel fat and ugly. No boys are interested in me. My schoolwork isn't very good. Girls in my class are so bitchy towards me. I feel ashamed of the way I look [f]

> I think I want to become anorexic because I am depressed about my weight...I am a little scared. I keep on having nightmares about becoming anorexic. I didn't eat anything today [f]

> I feel fat today. I want someone to cheer me up, a friend, someone to cuddle up to and say that I am not fat. I don't think that I am fat but everybody says I am [f]

> I really hate myself 'cause I am fat and ugly. I feel like killing myself sometimes 'cause I hate myself so much no-one loves me [f]

> I don't know what's wrong with me. I feel fat. I am going to go on a diet and then I will feel better about myself once I've lost a bit... I feel depressed. You know I just want to be happy like any other teenager girl but I can't. Somehow I just feeling boring and fat and no-one will want to know me shortly [f]

For some girls being fat is maybe not the issue. Rather they seem concerned about not being slim enough:

> I feel frustrated because I am not as thin as I want to be [f]

> I wish I was slimmer and nicer looking [f]

Only one boy talks of feeling fat:

> I hate being me. I feel as if I can't eat any sweets, cakes or any nice food because I keep thinking I am fat [m]

Both in these Howie Feel accounts and earlier in our questionnaire we see evidence of girls' concerns about their weight – in answer to the question 'things that make me feel unhappy about myself', over 10 per cent cite being overweight. These feelings may partly stem from girls' antipathy towards their maturing bodies and partly from living in a society which regards the slim/thin woman as ideal.

Earlier in this chapter we listed four other areas which seem to affect the the extent to which our teenagers value themselves. These categories are applicable to low self-esteem too – lack of social acceptance, lack of achievement or competence, lack of control and lack of 'virtue' can all damage self-esteem.

First then we see teenagers can feel bad about themselves when they believe that they are not fully accepted by their peers:

> I am a little worried because I do not seem to have many friends to hang around with. I think it is my fault as I do not like myself or my attitude towards others. I can't seem to change myself no matter how hard I try. I have not had a boyfriend for three years and I am desperate for someone

to get off with and cuddle. This won't happen as I am too ugly, fat and spotty. I have tried losing weight but it hasn't worked. I HATE ME!!! [f]

Right now I feel as if I don't fit in because I'm odd somehow. I feel no-one shares my interests or cares what I think. I keep asking myself questions and wondering if I'm normal or not. I feel as if I'm trapped somehow [f]

Some teenagers who feel they are not doing well in school take this to heart and label themselves in negative ways:

I feel that I am useless because I'm one of the dumbest in the class. I am ashamed of my marks [m]

Today I feel incredibly thick and stupid. I feel angry because everybody seems to be against me and people are always teasing me... All anyone talks about is how bad teenagers are today. Well things are harder now! [f]

Some talk of feeling that they lack control over their lives:

I really hate myself. I feel dead boring and I can't shape my life [m]

I am confused about my life because everything I do turns out a disaster [f]

Whereas 'being good' makes some feel pleased with themselves, the converse is also the case: some feel bad about themselves because they have not been good or have failed to conform or meet some moral ideal or standard.

I don't feel too good about myself because I should try harder to get on with people and do better work in class and not have too much carry on in my head [m]

I feel as if I have wronged myself. I keep getting into trouble at home. I have got a conduct card and keep forgetting to hand it in [m]

I'm very angry with myself because my mum trusts me and thinks I'm a very good boy, but I'm not. I smoke. I've been smoking for four years and I'm going to stop now [m]

I wish I had more money because I want to buy my dad and sister decent birthday presents. I hate how I steal rather than buy – I have stolen in the past tons of books from my local library. I regard myself as a good thief – never been caught. How long will it be? I have stolen off my parents – money. I feel terrible [m]

In this chapter we have seen examples of teenagers feeling good and feeling bad about themselves. These feelings are important and should not be disregarded. Feeling good about oneself is crucial to an overall sense of wellbeing. Furthermore, research has shown that there are several factors which appear to protect children and adolescents from mental health problems: self-esteem is one of these. In Chapter 16 Sally Butler considers how we can boost the self-esteem of young people and, in Chapter 17, George Potter discusses why and how schools should share in this responsibility.

CHAPTER 8

How We Feel About School

Given that the Howie Feel survey was carried out in the school setting, it is no surprise that school issues receive quite a lot of attention in the responses to the questionnaire.

One of the main 'tasks' for teenagers is to acquire an education, and, for most, this will happen in schools. Because parents and guardians of children are legally obliged to ensure this education is provided, young people have, in fact, little choice in the matter. As adolescence, in particular, is a time when young people want to assert their free will and decision making capabilities, tensions may arise.

In Chapter 1 we raised the fact that Howie Feel only gives us the views of the young people who were attending school that day – some pupils will have been off sick, truanting, or unable to take part because they had forgotten their consent form, etc. To gain a complete picture of teenagers and school life, the opinions of these young people should ideally be included.

Also, as for all the chapters on our data, we can only present what the young people *actually* choose to say and not what they *don't* say: if a pupil says school is boring, this does not necessarily mean that they find every single minute boring.

However, the fact that so many of the young people choose to reflect how they feel about school in 'Dear Diary' shows that school (where they can spend a large number of hours a week) plays an extremely prominent role in their lives and how they feel.

Positive feelings about school

Quite a few young people feel that school is 'OK' and write that they have no real problems in school. However, a few young people are more specific in revealing why they feel good about school:

I feel great today. I am coping well with the homework which there is a lot of! I get on well with most of my teachers which is great. I quite enjoy school [f]

School is always a difficult time for me because there is always tests, and the work is often very hard, but despite these points I find it quite enjoyable even it they do work me hard. I always go to school with a positive attitude, and today I am feeling both positive and feeling that I am just about coping with the world around me, even though sometimes I lack confidence and I get scared and disappointed, but I always try and feel good about the future and what it has in store for me [m]

Doing well in school

If we think back to the responses to 'things that make me feel good about myself', one in three young people identify doing well in school. The fact that doing well in school is important across *all* schools may seem remarkable to those who think young people in general are not interested in acquiring an education. As some of the 'Dear Diary' accounts suggest though, doing well can make young people feel great:

...in Chemistry I finally worked out how you form all these molecules and junk like that! Then in Maths I worked out something in a question that even the teacher didn't get. My day is going great so far [f]

I feel that I am doing well in school. I am getting good results in most subjects. In the rest I am improving nearly every day. I think I am quite brainy and very confident. I hope I keep this routine going and keep getting good results and hope things go my way and my sister does well too. I feel that tomorrow and in the future I will be a better person [m]

Doing well does not just relate to getting good marks or being top of the class. For some, coping with the workload and pressure of school feels good:

I felt depressed, under pressure as I had two exams last week, hundreds of homework. But I am feeling better now as I am coping with the work and have studied to the best of my ability [f]

Praise from teachers

The attitudes and actions of teachers in the classroom are a strong influence on how young people achieve in school (Rutter 1983). When those in authority give praise, young people feel confident and good about themselves and enjoy what they are doing. Those teenagers who write positively about their teachers relate this to when they receive praise:

> Today I feel quite happy because on the tanoy they said 'Well done' to the under 14's netball team [f]

> In geography I found out that the teacher liked my work so I felt even happier and proud [m]

Clearly, young people value positive feedback from teachers.

A place to meet friends

Because most young people spend a lot of their time in school, it is natural that friendships will be made between pupils. As we shall see in Chapter 10, friends can help cushion the stresses and strains of school life and, perhaps, make school a more interesting place to be:

> I've got Chemistry (I love it because I can talk to Craig, Paul and Tim through it), Computing (my friend Maggie sits next to me so I can talk to her) and French (Andy's there and he's hilarious). The best bit about school is the lunch break because I get to hang around with all my friends and we just have a laugh [f]

Friends can have a great influence on how young people get on in school. If being in a class with friends makes lessons more enjoyable, this may have implications for the way pupils should be assigned into classes, or even small groups during a class activity.

Liking Subjects

The remaining issue which contributes to whether the young people are enjoying school relates to specific class subjects. Some of the pupils talk of having 'good' subjects on the day of the questionnaire:

> Today I feel happy, sort of I don't know why but I do. My timetable is quite good so this has a little to do with how I feel [m]

> Today I feel good about a lot of things like my classes and in English we are reading a book and it is quite good [f]

What makes some subjects more enjoyable than others is up for debate. It seems likely that doing well in the subject, getting positive feedback from the teacher and having friends in the class will all play a part.

Negative feelings about school

Of those 'Dear Diary' accounts which relate to school issues, the majority contain negative feelings about certain aspects of school life. This does not automatically mean that all of the teenagers don't like school. When reading the accounts that follow, we must be aware of potential biases that may lead to so many teenagers making negative comments. Perhaps such feelings are easier to express than positive ones, or come into their minds more readily. Also, the comments which they make tend to be quite specific about certain aspects of the school setting and, therefore, we cannot necessarily generalise about how the young people feel about school as a *whole*.

Despite these considerations, young people are expressing very *real* feelings about school issues, all of which are valid. For many, school can be a mundane and miserable place.

Boredom

Perhaps it won't astonish us that the most commonly written phrase about school is 'boring'. A few hint at why this is the case:

> Every day I wake up and get ready for school, go to school, come home from school then go to bed etc. I want a change, something different to do (I'm bored with my life) [f]

> I feel bored, today has just been a very boring day, everything seems so long, there is no buzz about the place [m]

This last account gives a clear sense that school feels pretty lifeless and dull. In fact, a few young people contrast this tedium with life outside school:

> I am very bored. I wish I didn't have to go to school. School is very depressing although you learn stuff. The only good thing about it is playtime, dinnertime and home time and that's all [m]

> I feel bored, depressed and fed up with school, but I am happy, cheerful, lively and on top of the world at home time and lunch time because I hate school but I am coping very well with work and I am very happy because I can go out to play after school [m]

> I wish that the school would blow-up and I would be on holiday forever [f]

For some, life outside of school allows them to cope with the daily grind:

> I love weekends and live for weekends and holidays. I get through the week by thinking about the weekends [f]

A stressful place to be

A few young people describe feelings of stress at school:

> I feel very tired. I know school is a great thing and it helps you a lot but as I'm getting older I am under a lot of pressure and stress. I have not

been having a great social life. I feel as through I want to do well at school (really well) but there is too much to cope with [m]

I feel like I want to leave school for a while so that I can relax because I am so tense and then come back and start over again. To put it bluntly, Diary, I've had better days [f]

Today I feel stressed about school, I do not feel what I am doing is worth the effort [m]

For some, these feelings of stress relate to feeling confined by school and their lack of say in school matters:

Every morning apart from Saturday and Sunday I need to get up for school and I get angry. I get bored with near enough all the subjects in the school because I don't like the teachers. I feel as if I am trapped because I have no choice in the matter about going to school. If I had my own way I wouldn't go near school [m]

This morning I just felt like staying in bed because I had school. The thought of school just makes me feel fed up and bored. I wished I was sick so I didn't have to go. It felt like everything was on top of me because I had homework. I felt trapped because I have to go to school and I have to do everything asked of me [m]

Tests and exams

The most stressful experience by far for young people in school is exam time:

Today has not been particularly great I have just failed my Modern Studies test and I have so much revision to do for about 6 tests. Sometimes I wish I was a care-free little kid again so I wouldn't have all this pressure to do well all the time [f]

Today I feel very stressed and under pressure. I have to learn so much in such a short time and I seem to be getting one test after another. My mum is always telling me to just do my best but I always feel I should do better for her and me. I used to be a happy, cheerful person, now I just pretend I am [f]

Living up to the expectations of others can make exam pressure much worse:

I feel like everyone expects me to do really well in tests and stuff and if I don't, I feel ashamed of myself. I feel like I have to do better than my friends in tests because then I will still be liked. I think most of my friends feel like that too! [f]

> We have exams this term and I have to do well. I am nervous and scared I'll let everyone down. I am getting a lot of pressure at home at the moment to work and as of this I feel tense not that I'm planning anything stupid. Tomorrow will be better [f]

One girl feels that the time waiting for results just prolongs the anxiety:

> I think the teachers should mark them as soon as possible so we do not need to wait worrying for ages [f]

If many young people of this age group are already feeling under pressure about exams, we must consider what level of stress will they encounter in the years of formal exams (Standard Grades/Highers, etc). In Chapter 15 we will see that young people can feel overwhelmed by such anxieties, as they move up through the school system.

Homework

Although there is no legal precedent that requires young people to do homework, it is generally viewed by schools as an important part of the educational process. However, young people in our survey do not share this 'vision'. Whether we view homework as a necessary evil or something which interferes with the natural impulses of youth is another matter. Perhaps it is the fact that 'free time' must be sacrificed that makes the notion of homework so off-putting for so many teenagers – one in seven young people in our survey specifically say it is something which makes them unhappy:

> I don't think we should get homework because we want to have some fun in our lives after school instead of sitting in and doing work [m]

> When I get home, I am expected to get nagged at to study all day long, so I feel as if I do not have any freedom to be with my friends. OK my marks may be bad but this studying is ridiculous, at five hours a day or more, plus homework which takes one-and-a-half hours [m]

Others share this concern over how much time homework actually takes. In fact, most accounts relating to homework do, in one way or another, reflect the sheer amount handed out:

> I feel tired and bored today I have too much homework and mum will make me do it as soon as I get home. I wish I could have more time to do my homework. If I don't have enough time to do my homework teachers always get angry and moan. I am really sick of people moaning at me it starts to really get you down [f]

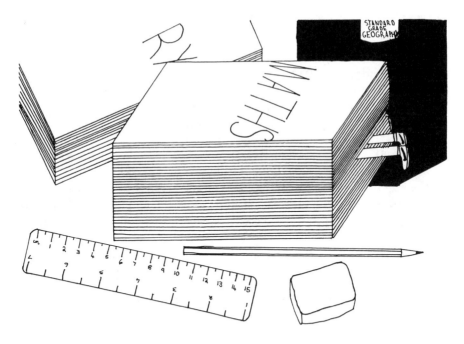

Figure 8.1 *Iain Mullin*

Some of the young people feel that the amount of homework handed out is caused by teachers not communicating with each other – that is, they give out work without considering what other homework commitments the pupils have:

> Today I feel cramped. I've too much homework, just a bit was a Chemistry test and two English essays. I wish the teachers from all the subjects would work out when to give things like tests, investigations, etc. so that they don't overlap [m]

> Today I feel stressed as homework can, at times, be too much for me. Some teachers, of course, give homework for the wrong night as we seem to have too much for that night. Last night I spent over four hours on homework, when we are to do only about two hours [m]

There are some instances where tensions about homework spill over into home life:

> You have a teacher moan at you all day long and when you go home your Mum will shout at you to do your homework. I think homework should be done in school so we don't get yelled at in the house [f]

Teachers

Along with exams and homework, teachers receive their fair share of negative press in the 'Dear Diary' accounts. As we mentioned earlier in this chapter, teachers' attitudes towards their pupils have an important effect on the progress of the pupils through the school system. In the 'Dear Diary' accounts, we see that the negative comments and criticisms made by teachers are often taken to heart, especially in those instances where there is a sense of injustice or of being 'pigeon-holed':

> Just now I am sitting in English feeling very angry. I always seem to get picked on by this teacher, if everyone's forgot something or didn't do something she just picks on me even just for the simplest little thing. She screams at me in a horrible high pitched voice which just goes right through me. I haven't been given a fair chance since I've been back from the holidays, obviously my second year teacher had said something bad about me because I did mess about in second year [m]

> Well I had a rubbish day today my maths teacher still hates me and gets me into trouble for nothing. This gets me angry. He's sexist as anything towards the girls. One girl forgot her homework six times and got nothing. One boy forgot his homework once and got a detention. Sexist prat. This makes me mad [m]

Teachers can certainly stir up strong feelings in their pupils:

> It's the way they say they give us enough sex education when they don't. It's the way in which they treat boys differently from the girls. It's the way in which they do not warn us about drugs at my age. They = Adults, Teachers, Parents [f]

> I hate saying Sir. As if an old prick who has a degree needs to be called sir. Sometimes I contemplate confronting him, but I have to keep in with him or my life is a mess [m]

> My teacher said that I was a failure because I didn't understand [m]

> In maths the teacher was shouting at me because I couldn't understand a sum he asked me I felt really upset, I don't want to go into maths again [f]

A few of the young people reflect on how teachers and pupils communicate, and hint at some of the obstacles to this interaction:

> I feel that the teachers should have more of a sense of humour. I think that punishment exercises should be destroyed and that teachers should also listen to the pupils, just like we have to listen to them [m]

> School can be annoying because sometimes the teachers just can't seem to understand us [f]

> I also hate having a male guidance teacher because I cannot talk to him [f]

One pupil does not lay the blame solely at the teachers' door however:

> Sometimes I feel depressed because of the attitude of some teachers and pupils at school. I would like it if nobody ever fell out with each other [f]

Although we see a number of negative comments in relation to teachers and their practices, we must temper this with the fact that many of the accounts focus on very specific events and feelings. What is clear, however, is that pupils pick up feelings from teachers very easily and are sometimes deeply affected by what is said in a classroom.

Disliking subjects

Just as some of the young people feel they have good subjects, others are not so happy with their timetable:

> I am sitting in English and it is boring, it is a crap subject 'cause all you do is write and you don't get a laugh [gender unknown]

> Today I feel bad because the subjects in my timetable are all set out badly. The day I have has a lot to do with how I feel [m]

> I feel like collapsing because I have to stand a full period in Technical [f]

> Today I do not feel good because I get double Maths and double French. I do not like these subjects so I feel bored and confused because I am not very good at them [m]

This last account suggests, perhaps, that young people who find subjects difficult may come to dislike them. Also, if young people do not enjoy their classes, how likely are they to do well in them?

Doing Badly in School

In Chapter 4 we see that the most common response to 'three things that make me feel bad about myself' is doing badly at school, with one in four young people responding in this way. Although most of the young people do not choose to discuss this in 'Dear Diary', a few brave souls talk of their feelings towards this:

I feel that I am useless because I am one of the dumbest in my class. I am ashamed of my marks [m]

I wish I could just get away. I feel so depressed. I just can't cope with the work at school, suicide would be the easiest thing. I hate my life! [f]

Others in school

We have seen earlier that school can bring teenagers into contact with those they like. It can also bring then into contact with those they don't:

I like school but I don't like the people in it [m]

I sometimes have a hard time at school. I can do work okay, it's just that some people treat me as if I'm stupid. It's as if I'm subordinate at times [m]

I can't do much work in my class because some of the boys don't like working and keep interrupting the teacher when she goes over the work for our test [m]

Peer relationships will be picked up and put under the microscope in Chapter 10.

Mixed feelings about school

For most young people it is likely that their experiences of school life have ups and downs, rather than being wholly positive or negative. The final accounts we present represent those who express mixed feelings about school:

Some days I feel trapped. Homework sometimes gets on top of me but I still find a way to do it. Some days I feel great, I play football and if I'm lucky I score a goal and sometimes I just can't be bothered. Some days school is great and it goes in fast. Some days it's rubbish and it goes very, very, very slow. Some days the teachers seem to be on your back and other days they help you a lot. Some days I'm angry at my sisters and some days I don't annoy them [m]

First period I felt happy, second period I felt bored, third period I felt scared, fourth period I felt bored [m]

Even when they are not happy about certain aspects of school, the fact that schooling can provide a gateway into employment is not far from some minds:

I don't really like maths but I suppose I will just have to do it if I want to do my best and get a job [m]

I am a bit depressed about my school work today. I need to work harder, if I don't I might not get a job. I just feel that I have to wake up to myself [m]

In this chapter we have come across a wide range of emotions relating to the school experience. In Chapter 17 George Potter reflects on the implications of these data on teaching practices, and indeed the whole structure of schooling, as he perceives it from his experience as a teacher.

CHAPTER 9

How We Feel About Our Families

Politicians today are constantly reminding us of the importance of family values and the family institution is often held up to be the backbone of society. What happens within the confines of the family unit is seen to have far-reaching consequences for events outside this relationship and the press seem eager to find evidence of the effects on society of the 'breakdown' of family life.

The family environment certainly has an impact on the emotional lives of family members. Families play an important role, for instance, in supporting their teenagers from the dependency of childhood to the independence of adulthood. This transition requires that all family members (not just the adolescent) must redefine their roles. Such 'tweaking' of relationships can affect family dynamics because parents and teenagers must come to terms with changing expectations of one another.

Despite the potential for tensions over this period of transition, research would suggest that families *in general* cope well with these adjustments and most report healthy relationships during and after these times (Offer, Ostrov and Howard 1981). It would seem that problems which do occur tend to relate to everyday events – squabbles over whose turn it is for the dishes and which T.V. channel to watch. These problems will inevitably arise when people live in close proximity to one another. However, whilst teenagers can have grievances about their parents, these grievances are not seen to undermine their relationship as a whole and can usually be resolved (Steinberg 1988). Throughout our questionnaire the family is frequently mentioned in positive ways – this no doubt includes the 18 per cent who choose to circle 'loved' in the Field Of Words. It is worth keeping this in mind when we reflect on some of the 'Dear Diary' accounts.

We must also be aware that notions of what constitute 'family' vary enormously and we must consider all sorts of family make-ups (including step-families, single parent families, extended families, etc). Given the high rate of divorce and family break-ups, many teenagers nowadays have to negotiate

Figure 9.1   *Karyn McNaught*

relationships with new families – step-parents, stepbrothers and sisters, etc. Such complex relationships are reflected in our teenagers' accounts.

In 'Dear Diary', when teenagers talk about their families – in particular their parents – often they tend to do so in negative ways. This may be viewed as young people having a natural moan at adults who impose rules and restrictions on them and not as indicative of deeper problems with the parent-teenage relationship (Steinberg 1988). Nevertheless, we cannot trivialise these feelings and dismiss them as unimportant. Furthermore, a number of the teenagers may well be experiencing grave difficulties with their family relationships. Whether the problems presented may be viewed as 'serious' or 'trivial' to us as adults, we feel they are all valid and should be given credence. Of course, we also recognise that the task of parenting is far from being an easy one and, at times, can be a stressful and frustrating experience. Unfortunately our Howie Feel survey only lets us look at the views from one side of the picture. Perhaps the future will allow us a chance to hear the voices of parents.

Positive feelings about family

We should recall that, earlier in the questionnaire, one in six young people choose to mention their families as sources of happiness. In 'Dear Diary', some teenagers write with warmth and affection about their families:

> I have got a great family, a great home and great friends too! [m]

> I like it when I go out with my family and whenever I am with them [m]

> I can't wait to get home and see my Mum's cheery face [f]

Some teenagers specifically mention parents and sound pleased to have the parents that they do:

> I have to go to my Drama rehearsals tonight so that will get me out for a while. My Mum and Dad walk me there. They are great parents! [m]

> My Mum and I are like good friends [f]

> I feel loved because I know that my family and friends love me and care for me [f]

Feeling loved and valued by their families give some a sense of stability and security:

> I also feel that I am lucky to have such a lovely family and that is one of the reasons that I feel good about the future [m]

> I am coping with life because my parents encourage me to tell them if I have any problems and this makes me feel loved [m]

We read accounts from a few teenagers who express their desire and satisfaction in pleasing their parents:

> I want to please my parents and do well [f]

> Today my computing teacher told me I was in a Credit computing class, that made me feel very happy and made my parents proud [f]

Not only do young people talk about their parents, some also write of close relationships with brothers and sisters:

> Everything's good at home and me, my sister and brother are all close and I'm getting on really well with my sister's boyfriend [f]

> My little brother has come to this school, I hang around with him now. I like him more and more... We are close to each other but we fight with each other but we have set a goal for us to stop [m]

Clearly, siblings can be an important source of friendship for young people. Although the extended family crops up throughout the questionnaire, only a couple of teenagers make positive comments about them in 'Dear Diary':

> I think I feel happy because my Gran's getting out of hospital today but she is going to be in a wheelchair for the rest of her life [f]

> My uncle is my favourite person because he is really funny [f]

Negative feelings about family

Arguments

As touched on earlier, family life through the teenage years does not necessarily live up to its reputation as a time of all-out war. However, the early years of adolescence are often characterised by an increase in squabbles between parents and teenagers. Although these are often about 'minor issues', they can, nevertheless, feel distressing for all concerned:

> I wish my parents would stop blaming me for everything and leave me alone [f]

> I don't feel very good with myself today because last night I had a fight with my Mum. Mum and Dad were fighting last night and I told them to stop shouting. Then my Mum started shouting at me saying that I should just shut up and get out of her face. So I went and sat in the toilet. I was thinking about what I would have said if she had said anything to me. I kept thinking that she would have came up and made up with me but she didn't. I didn't say anything to her this morning and I'm dreading going home [f]

Mum's constant nagging and fussing and complaining is getting me down a bit but I'll manage. She claims I've changed but I don't know how I've become changed, and I don't know how I've become secretive as she says I have [m]

Mum was nice to me in the car going to school, giving me compliments. At first I was pleased but I remembered she always does that and then moans at me, then she is nice to me and then she lets me down again and moans at me. So I try not to like her a lot because it upsets me more when she does moan when I really like her [f]

Lack of freedom

Because adolescents are neither the child of their past nor the adult of the future there is an obvious dilemma as to which role they should play. Most of the negative accounts reflecting family issues relate to this predicament, whereby the young people strive to be accepted as independent adults in an environment which they believe still views them as children:

At the moment I would love to run away and get away from everything. I want to escape from my parents telling me what to do and constantly trying to rule my life. I hate them, it's as though my Mum doesn't want to let me have any fun. She says she knows what it is like to be 14 but I don't think she does, she couldn't possibly. She thinks the easiest thing to do is to ground me at night but she doesn't understand that the more she does that, the worse I am going to be and the more I am going to hate her. I just want to kill myself sometimes. I wish something or someone would make everything alright. When I had been arguing with my boyfriend and my parents I just felt like killing myself, it was as though nobody would even notice or care. I hoped that they'd hate themselves for causing me to do this and I hoped that their lives would always be as miserable as mine always seems to have been. I wish I could get away. I just feel so depressed [f]

I want to leave school next year but my parents won't let me. They won't let me go out, baby sit. All I ever hear is maybe next year, you're too young. Well stuff them, it's my life. I am going to do it my way [f]

I am depressed because I am not allowed to hang about with my new group of friends outside school anymore because they are a 'bad influence'... My parents think locking me up will solve the problem but they are just making me lie to them more [f]

I am not very happy today and haven't been for a while. Recently I have been arguing with my Mum about everything. She is always moaning at

Figure 9.2   *Jeremy Curran*

me and I feel she doesn't trust me. I go out every night with my friends and when I go home my Mum questions me about everything. I am going out with a boy from school but I don't think my Mum trusts me. I am fed up with school and my house. I need a break from things. I feel trapped because every day is the same and in my Mum's eyes I can't do anything right. Sometimes I feel the whole world is against me. The only thing that cheers me up is going out with my friends but my mum can't see that [f]

Being a teenager is hard. Your parents are always on at you and if you don't do well you feel as if you have let them down. Everyone is on at you to be nice and to do what is right. You've not to do anything wrong, but it is hard sometimes. It is hard to always do what your parents would want you to do. You have to try things out for yourself, not to be told don't do this because you need to try things. It feels as if everyone is always putting pressure on you and are taking control of your life. I don't like this. I need to be in control but sometimes when I can't be in control of my opinions I try to control other things. I don't think it is fair to rule other people's lives. [f]

Interestingly, the accounts suggest that this feeling of being over-protected is a bigger issue for girls than boys. It's maybe that girls are more restricted in terms of what they are and are not allowed to do, or that they just are more likely to notice it. Remember, girls talk of 'going out' as something which makes them happy (more so than boys) and thus may be more likely to be affected by restrictions. Parents might also perceive that girls are more vulnerable than boys and need to be looked after more, protected from the possibilities of teenage pregnancies, violence and the like. However, several teenagers recognise that such over-protection can be well-intentioned:

My parents can be a real pain sometimes and over-protective but that is only because they love me and I love them [f]

In Chapter 16 Sally Butler reflects on the fragmented nature of adolescents' lives. Becoming an independent adult may involve teenagers choosing to keep some of their lives private, or at least free from parental scrutiny. A few young people talk of their resentment when their privacy is invaded:

I also feel loved by my parents but feel they do not give me privacy all of the time. They like to always know what I'm doing every minute of the day [f]

I don't know if I am going to keep writing my diary because I caught Mum reading it the other night. No-one seems to respect my privacy, even though I'm a teenager. Folk just won't leave me alone [f]

Privacy is an important issue for everyone, but may be especially so for the developing teenager. Clearly, parents are faced with the dilemma of wishing to protect their children whilst allowing them to develop an independent identity. Maybe we adults should consider how we would feel if *our* parents wanted to keep tabs on us every minute of the day?

Parents don't understand

According to research, the notion that there is a large 'generation gap' between young people and their parents is more than likely exaggerated. In fact, adults and their teenagers have very similar views and attitudes (Youniss and Smollar 1985). However, we find that some young people feel that they are not being understood by their parents, sometimes because they are not being listened to:

> I feel a bit stressed about going home because my mum doesn't know what it is like to be me. She thinks everything is easy but it is not [f]

> I wish my Mum and Dad would listen to me and not keep having arguments with me and blaming me for everything [f]

> My Mum has been frustrating me, she thinks she knows how to talk to me because she is a counsellor. She is so patronising and she only wants to know what I am doing that I shouldn't. She thinks that stuff I do is a cry for help but she doesn't know what it is like and she doesn't ask...I wish I could talk to my mother without her criticising me [f]

Before those of us who are parents of teenagers begin to despair at never being on the same wavelength as them, we must look back and recall that approximately one in four young people state they can talk to their Mum about their feelings and one and six that they can talk to their parents.

Pressure to do well

Young people feel pressure to do well from all sorts of quarters. Although parents who take an interest in their teenager's academic performance are trying to serve their son's or daughter's best interest, for some teenagers this 'support' can feel overwhelming:

> I feel scared because I know if I fail my test which I probably will, my parents will compare me to my older sister who is much more clever and confident than me [f]

> I've got a test today, keep worrying about it. Don't know what my parents would say if I messed up, so I won't tell them. It's hard living up to the expectations of parents [m]

Parents not caring

Just as a few young people talk of feeling loved by their families, there are a similar number who write of feeling rejected:

> I have to move house because of my selfish Dad and his bitch girlfriend...
> I feel rejected by my father and boys in general...I wish my Dad would phone [f]

> Parents argue with me everyday and put me down. Nobody cares... I feel as if I want my own space. Everyone has to criticise me in some way. People make me look small, especially grown ups [f]

> I had a fight with my Dad last night. I drove away his girlfriend apparently although I didn't mean to. I wish my parents were still married and loved each other. He was shouting at me and said 'what do I get out of you being alive?'... Anyway I am absolutely positive, completely sure that he would never hurt me, but what he said kind of threw me a bit [f]

When we consider that family warmth and compassion can help young people to cope with life and its difficulties, we must recognise that we all have a part to play in making young people feel valued. This final account also illustrates the power of language and makes us think of all those things that we have said in the heat of the moment.

Other family worries

In addition to those accounts which reflect parent–teenager relationships, a number of young people write about wider family issues. In our survey, young people seem to carry many 'adult worries' on their shoulders. One particular area of concern is parental discord:

> Home is OK but Mum and Dad aren't getting on very well at the moment and it is all for stupid reasons which don't seem important to me. I don't understand why people can't get along and try to reason with one another [f]

> I am a little stressed with my parents arguing. I can't tell anyone how I feel about it because I know they'd laugh. I am sure it will all stop soon though [m]

> ...I am also confused and scared in case my parents split up [f]

Young people also have worries about their parents' welfare:

> ...once or twice I have thought of running away, but it is the way my mother would act. She wouldn't sleep until I was found [m]

I wish I could help my Dad. I feel so sorry for him. I'm a bit sad and angry too. I don't know if I can tell my pals about this thing [f]

Some teenagers also have specific worries concerning their parents' financial situation:

My parents stopped arguing but they still won't talk. It was my birthday the night they started arguing, it was about money spent on the house [m]

I am scared. I am scared that my Mum and Dad have not got enough money. We have a lovely house but seem to have no spare money for Christmas [f]

I also feel troubled because of the problems in the house. We are getting bills every day and because Xmas is coming up things are getting worse and I keep thinking that we would be getting kicked out of the house but it's never going to happen, but it just keeps coming into my head [gender unknown]

Illness/death in family

The loss of anyone close to us through illness and death is devastating at any time and in adolescence the trauma of the loss of loved ones can be particularly hard. As well as coming to terms with their own loss they may encounter grieving parents, brothers and sisters and others whom they would normally rely upon for support and comfort. Death and illness feature in response to the question 'things that make me unhappy' and we also see examples of young people's responses to these events in 'Dear Diary':

I feel very very sad today because my Aunt died on Sunday. It makes me feel depressed because I can't stop thinking about it, and when I think about it I start to cry. I feel that nobody else would understand how I am feeling. My friends are wondering what is wrong with me and they are thinking that they have done something wrong [gender unknown]

Living with Grandpa for the past 10 years has been difficult and it's getting worse as he goes on at everyone because of his depression. This hurts my Mum and I feel sorry for this. We all cope though [m]

A few young people express their fear of the unknown:

Life scares me a lot because when I wake up in the morning and see my parents it makes me happy but when I leave for school in the morning that could be the last time I ever see them because something could happen to them or me [f]

Others in family

Although brothers and sisters can be a good source of friendship for some young people, many complain about difficulties in their sibling relationships:

> I come home from school, my brothers shout and punch me, then I have my homework to do. This is my basic typical day [f]

> My sisters are really annoying me and I hate it. I never get any time or peace to do any homework or study [f]

> I feel sick and tired and disinterested because my brother broke my video cabinet and I told him to stay out but he doesn't and my Mum does nothing to help [m]

> Today I don't know how I feel. I change every five minutes, my life is very weird. Ever since my little sister was born three weeks ago I have been thrown aside. I get really upset nobody has time for me [f]

Although research suggests that teenagers in *general* experience good relationships with their families, Howie Feel shows that even minor difficulties can give rise to feelings of distress – probably for parents too. In Chapter 18 Mary Ross explores the nature of parent–teenager relationships and offers some solutions to the types of tensions that have been raised in this chapter.

CHAPTER 10

How We Feel About Our Peers

It has been estimated that even if you discount the hours spent in class lessons, teenagers spend about twice as many waking hours with their peers as with their parents and other adults. In fact, for teenagers, the largest single category of 'significant others' are peers of the same sex as themselves (Csikszentmihalyi and Larson 1984).

The importance of adolescent peer groups may stem, in part, from efforts to cope with the structure of secondary schools. Moving from primary to secondary school usually requires pupils to cope with a flood of new faces, whilst at the same time adjusting to a new and looser form of supervision from teachers. At primary school children tend to have the same teacher for most of the day on most days, whereas at secondary school the contact time with individual teachers is far shorter. By being part of a group, individuals are protected from having to navigate alone the uncharted territory of a new school and a sea of unfamiliar faces.

The fact that this chapter is so long reflects the frequency with which boys and girls talk about their peer group – most commonly referring to those with whom they 'hang around', that is their cliques.

Positive feelings about peers

Friendships

Many young people reflect on the benefits of their friendships:

> The thing that makes me happier is the thought of going home and then meeting with my friends and doing something exciting. If I didn't have any friends I think I wouldn't have a life. It's my friends that make me feel good in the morning when I wake up and make me do things that I haven't done before, like going to places I didn't know existed. It's good to have friends and it's good to be happy [gender unknown]

Having friends or feeling part of a group seems to be valued by both girls and boys:

> I feel happy because my friends are there [f]

> I feel happy because I have a lot of friends just now that are alright [m]

> I feel in a good mood because I am in the right crowd [m]

For many, negative feelings about coming to school are offset by seeing friends there:

> This morning I didn't want to come to school but when I got to school I felt better when I seen my friends [m]

Both boys and girls talk about friends making them feel good about themselves:

> Today when I woke up at 7.00 a.m. I felt tired and lonely when everyone else got up and there was no-one around. I packed for school and felt bored as I waited around. When I arrived at school I felt cheerful and important as my friends were all there, and quite confident for the day to come [f]

> I always feel good about myself when I am around my friends. Also my girlfriend. I wish my mum would talk to me the way my friends do but it's impossible [m]

> I feel good about myself because I have hundreds of pals [m]

Many teenagers highlight the fun of 'having a laugh':

> Today I feel very hyper, excited and happy. This is because we were dancing about in changing rooms and we got everyone singing and it was funny [f]

Both boys and girls write about enjoying going out with their friends:

> I'm going to stay over at my friend's house on Saturday and we're going to the Sub Club! I can't wait [f]

More interestingly perhaps are the clear qualitative *differences* emerging between those friendships held by boys and by girls. For instance, 'talking' is a recurring feature in the girls' accounts of their friendships:

> My friends come up for me. On the way we talked about many things, boys, school, leisure, etc [f]

Whereas both genders enjoy 'having a laugh', we get the impression that for girls this is often rooted within the context of their conversations, whereas for boys this is more akin to joking or fooling around.

I had a laugh with my friends at interval. We talked about our Mums and Dads and life in general [f]

I got up this morning to be woken again my mother arguing but I shrugged it off and went to meet my pals who at least gave me a chance to laugh [m]

Support

A very large number of girls emphasise the emotional support which they derive from their friends:

I had a good day at school because I seen all my friends and talked to them about the things that was bothering me [f]

The way I feel is like topping myself but I know I won't 'cos my friend will stop me. If it wasn't for her I would already [f]

Some girls also identify ways in which their friendships are qualitatively different from their other relationships:

I feel happy and cheerful because I have got my friends to give me a laugh, and my parents to give me a good life [f]

At times I feel I have no-one to talk to because I don't want any teachers to put me down, and I don't talk to my parents as I feel uncomfortable. I talk to my best friend and she is great [f]

Sometimes the sort of support provided is that of advice:

Last night my boyfriend and I had an argument and now we're split up. We asked a couple of friends what they thought and they said we should just be friends because I really like him a lot and I know he likes me [f]

Others talk of the ability of their friends to cheer them up:

Today I feel happy and energetic because all my friends have cheered me up. At 8.30 I left the house in a bad mood and got the bus to school, when I got to school my friends were laughing so I joined in and now I am happy [f]

Got to school and was told that the B.C.G. vaccination was next week. I was really scared. But then I saw my best friend and a smile was put upon my face [f]

In sharp contrast to the girls, it is extremely uncommon for boys to either reflect on the quality of their friendships or to say that their male friends give them emotional support. Typically, the sorts of positive things they say about their friends are along the following lines:

> I am feeling very good. Nobody is bothering me…all my friends are talking to me [m]

> I feel good to be me today because I have no enemies and have no problems with school apart from when I get into trouble. I live a pretty basic life for a male and I get up to all the tricks too. I have a bit of a carry on now and again [m]

However, although in the minority, a small number of boys *do* talk of valuing the support which their friends offer:

> A lot of the time my family don't understand my needs or my taste in music, so I can't turn to them for help. My friends are the ones who understand me so I feel sorry for the 'nae pals' [m]

> I feel fine today. I have been talking to my friends and everything seems okay so far. If it wasn't for my good friends I wouldn't be coping so well. I always want to be with them and talk to them I don't know where I would be without them [m]

> My friends stick up for me and I don't make fun of them [m]

It seems then that loyalty ('my friends stick up for me') and intimacy ('I can talk to my friends about how I feel') are highly valued in teenage friendships, particularly amongst girls. Research elsewhere supports the gender differences we see here, showing that girls regard their friendships as offering more intimacy and emotional support. However, not only are girls more likely to disclose personal issues but they are also more inclined to try and meet the emotional needs of their friends (Younnis and Smollar 1985). In the Howie Feel accounts there is a distinct sense of empathy in many girls' accounts, often with the emotional lives of many girls being enmeshed with those of their friends. For instance, many talk of feeling happy when their friends are happy:

> It's my friend's birthday and she liked the present I got her. I was happy. When she's cheerful, it makes me cheerful also [f]

> All my friends are getting boyfriends and I am pleased for them [f]

Girls also talk of their capacity and satisfaction in being able to buck up their friends:

> I was very happy when I went out with my friends tonight. My friend was feeling down. So me being so happy cheered her up too. I feel on top of the world. It feels good to be me [f]

> I'm glad because if I'm in a good mood then if my friends are depressed I can make them in a good mood [f]

> Today I helped someone with their mixed up feelings and that made me
> feel really useful to someone who needs help [f]

This altruism sometimes involves offering others 'permission to speak':

> I don't like people to be unhappy as I feel it will have an effect on me.
> If someone were feeling sad I would ask them what the problem was and
> might try and make them happy [f]

Because we witness qualitative differences in the styles of interaction in girls
and in boys, this does not necessarily mean that the *substance* or quality of boys'
relationships is inferior; rather, it may be that boys experience closeness through
sharing activities (e.g. football) rather than through sharing their innermost
thoughts.

Contrary to the empathy and concern we have seen above, some teenagers'
comments can be described as '*schadenfreude*' – a German term which refers to
the satisfaction derived from learning of another's misfortune:

> Today I feel happy because nobody has teased me... At lunchtime my
> friend were arguing with someone and it was very funny. That made me
> feel good because it wasn't me that the other person was arguing with
> [f]

> I am looking forward to going to football training tonight and also
> looking forward to Sunday because my team are playing a team whom
> I know a lot of players, and I am slagging them saying we are going to
> thrash them. I feel good [m]

Negative feelings about peers

So far we have seen that our teenagers seem to enjoy and value many features
of friendships or cliques. However, these positive aspects represent only one
side of the coin. On the flip side, friendships and cliques bring problems. For
instance, in their relationships, children learn not only how to get along but
also how to reject or exclude others and such intimate friendships can give rise
to insecurity, jealousy and resentment (Rubin 1980). These, and a whole range
of other negative emotions, surface frequently in the Howie Feel diaries.

In the first half of the chapter we saw that when the teenagers talk in positive
terms, their remarks relate to their relationships with their friends or cliques.
In contrast to this, when our teenagers talk about being unhappy, they refer
both to their immediate friends or cliques, and also to their wider group of
peers.

> I feel fine but sometimes it is hard for me to understand what the problem
> is with the other kids. They seem to have an attitude problem and seem
> to think that they have to prove themselves to each other. I think it's

wrong. Luckily I am not like them. I am not brainy nor dumb. I am just a normal human being [f]

Why can't I just be accepted by the group? Why do they always take the rip out of me? [m]

Friendship difficulties

Many girls write about friendship difficulties. The fact that they talk about tensions gives the impression that they are easily bruised by the comments and behaviours of their peers. Perhaps this is an inevitable consequence of the intimate nature of their friendships:

My friend is being bitchy to my best friend. She takes days about. One day it's me she's bitchy to, the next it's my best friend. She really does my nut in [f]

I have been thinking about this friend I have but she doesn't go about with us and I used to tell her things that I wouldn't tell anyone else and I felt comfortable around her but she doesn't hang around with us anymore. I miss her [f]

My best friend has found someone better to hang out with… My best friend is really pretty and popular unlike me who is just plain and boring [f]

When we read these comments we see another feature recognised in adolescent friendships: the fact that rather than being constant, they are changing and dynamic. In addition to changes in who's friends with who, girls talk about very short-term ups and downs in their friendships:

Today I had an argument with friends. This made me feel really down, but now I am much better because I am talking to them again [f]

Today I feel happy and content. I don't know why as my friend got off with the boy I love but I love her too. I forgave her for it but she was crying [f]

Some of the girls describe seemingly complex relationships:

I wonder how it's gonna go today between me and my best friend and this other girl who's kind of her best friend, but she says she's my best friend too. I feel like there's always some stupid competition between me and this other girl which is just so annoying. She always copies her and agrees with anything she says just to get her attention [f]

A few girls and boys talk about feeling pulled between friends and having their loyalties challenged:

I feel angry because some of my friends aren't talking to each other and I am left in the middle. I feel cheated because the person who I thought was one of my best friends doesn't talk to me anymore [f]

My friends have fallen out and they said 'You either go about with him or us' and I don't want to fall out with him or them because I like them both [m]

Slagging

Many accounts featured the issue of 'slagging' – a colloquial term for 'making fun' of others. It is likely that slagging can serve several functions: it may enable teenagers to tease each other about sensitive issues without feeling that they will be held personally accountable for any hurtful comments; it may be used as a vehicle for displaying one's sense of humour, for flirting in a 'safe' manner or for boosting solidarity amongst friends. Or it may be about just being plain nasty.

Certainly, in the main, girls find slagging upsetting:

I feel sad when people slag me, and I feel like crying, and I don't think teachers take me seriously [f]

Because I am going out with Philip now I am getting slagged. I feel angry and embarrassed. I wish people would mind their own business [f]

Boys' responses to slagging are more variable than those of the girls. Whereas some find it upsetting, others turn the other cheek:

Quite a lot of the time I have dark eyes and people call me shady. I do not like this but I take it lightly [m]

[I am] tired and depressed. Want to batter people who slag me. Think I'll run away to anywhere. People who slag me are wee widos who need a wash. They are just wee attention seekers [m]

Today I have been slagged a few times but that's normal. Everyone gets slagged and slags someone sometime in the day [m]

People sometimes tease me because of my lack of experience with girls. This does not upset me because I do not care what other people think about me [m]

Jealousy

In earlier chapters we have seen that girls describe themselves as feeling jealous more frequently than boys do. In the 'Dear Diary' accounts a handful of boys and girls talk about feeling jealous of their peers:

I feel jealous. Everybody else's life seems so perfect [f]

I feel as though some people really hate me and are avoiding me… I'm jealous of the many people enjoying life. Sometimes I feel like ending my own life [m]

Feelings of jealousy are largely confined to those situations where girls are vying for boys' attention:

Today I feel like jumping off a building because the boy I fancy someone else does too but she shows that she does, but I don't, and it makes me feel like killing her but she is my friend. She knows I like him too but she likes him and she wants to go out with him. We are both jealous of each other [f]

We shall return to this jealousy in Chapter 11, which looks at teenagers and their 'romantic' involvements.

Broken rules

Adolescents often regard loyalty and intimacy as hallmarks of their friendships (Savin-Williams and Berdt 1990). It is, therefore, perfectly understandable that they feel aggrieved when these 'rules' are violated – a feeling which is expressed more by our girls than by our boys:

I feel very depressed because I keep getting slagged off because I asked out a boy and he said no because this girl told him things about me and said things about me… I felt really let down and I feel like I'm sick of my friends as they are the ones who are laughing at me. They're not really friends then [f]

I hate it how people hit me or make fun of me because I'm nothing, and if two of my friends are with me they block me out and talk amongst themselves, and if people make fun of me, they laugh at me, but after they try to be nice again as if nothing has happened [m]

I feel angry about the way my so called friends are behaving. I don't think they're good friends for behaving this way [f]

I'm unsure about friends at this school – have many but not quite as good as the old school. I don't think they're the forgiving and supportive type – more like just for the good times [m]

Some talk of being let down down and disappointed by their friends:

Today some of my friends were supposed to bring back some CDs that I have given them a loan of, but they didn't bring them so this made me feel as if they were not real friends and they fuck me about without thinking about how I feel [m]

I feel depressed, lonely and angry with my friends. Friends are supposed to respect you and just because I am clever they call me a swot. They think I am bad tempered and are always telling me to calm it or don't get hyper. Hearing this always makes me angry [f]

Similarly, a handful express their regrets over violating the trust which their friends bestow on them:

I feel really guilty for betraying a friend who thinks so highly of me. I took her diary and read it. She has not found out but when she discovered it was missing, she was going to cry [f]

Loyalty to friends also entails loyalty in their absence and a few write of being upset when others talk behind their backs. However, we are unable to discern whether these accounts relate to friends or to the wider peer group:

Today I found out that someone was talking about me. I felt on top of the world until I was told. My confidence was shattered [f]

I feel very uncomfortable today. I feel people are talking about me behind my back. I feel like that most days though. My friends are nice to me but sometimes they act weird around me. I don't understand. Sometimes I can't be bothered with life and my grades suffer [f]

Clearly then many hold a set of expectations about what friends are and how they should behave. Already we have suggested that some of these relate to loyalty issues. The other defining feature of adolescent friendships we mentioned was intimacy – the ability to share one's thoughts and feelings. Just as intimacy features prominently in girls' positive views, we find intimacy *problems* also emerge in their diaries:

I feel awful. I feel like my friends are just using me because I am smart and I help them with all their problems and work. I feel like they are only hanging around with me because they feel sorry for me but I can't say anything because no-one understands me, no-one ever has [f]

Today I feel happy and sad because sometimes I can tell someone my problems and they laugh – that is what makes me sad. What makes me happy today is when I told someone something and they did not laugh and listened [f]

Left out and lonely

By their very definition, the existence of cliques results in some people being excluded:

> In certain classes at school I feel left out because none of my friends are in it and everyone else in the class has their own friends... When I have friends in my class I tend to ignore everyone else because that's what they do to me [f]

Feelings of being left out are not restricted to those who have failed to become part of a crowd. Rather, those who have friends also talk of feeling excluded:

> I sometimes feel lonely as my friends do not include me in anything they are doing or going to do [f]

> I know I am probably over-reacting about this which I have a tendency to do, and I am paranoid and have no confidence in myself but now my two best friends are doing games at lunchtime and go around with others at lunch, and I think that they do not really want me there. I miss my old school so much even though it was three years ago. It only had 42 pupils altogether and everyone was like a family. You could never be depressed – everyone there was your friend [f]

In the examples above, the young people describe *episodes* of feeling excluded, that is such feelings are of a short-term nature and are restricted to particular situations. There are others for whom being left out appears to be a more chronic or ongoing problem. Some, mostly boys, talk of being unpopular or of feeling lonely and isolated:

> I wish I was dead because people do not like me, and all think I am poor, so if I felt very, very bad I would jump out my window. I hate my life [m]

> I feel very lonely, I haven't any pals. I have fell to pieces recently [m]

> I feel as though people really hate me and are avoiding me. I feel jealous because of the many people enjoying life. Sometimes I feel like ending my own life [m]

> Today I feel the same as every day – isolated from everyone else. Lisa always ignores me and talks to me when it suits her. I sometimes get called names by the boys. I know they are only kidding but it still hurts inside. I feel left out. No-one ever bothers to see what I am doing. I end up just tagging along with everyone else. I sometimes go to Avril for support in certain matters but she would rather talk to the boys. Hopefully she may realise I just want to be her friend [f]

> Today I feel lonely because I have no-one to talk to in class. Since 3rd year started all my friends are in different classes so I don't see them much. I wish I had someone to talk to and tell them how I feel [m]

Although adolescence is generally a time characterised by a high level of sociability, it can also be a time of extreme loneliness. It is important to recognise that merely being with others does not solve the problem:

> I feel very uncomfortable and unhappy. I feel on a different level from everyone else [m]

Research provides some evidence to suggest that those teenagers who feel lonely engage in the same number of social interactions as their more sociable-feeling peers. However those who report feeling lonely also report less warmth and intimacy in their 'friendships' (Jones 1981). The feelings of loneliness we see in the Howie Feel accounts then may (at least in part) reflect feelings of dissatisfaction with the level of intimacy which some teenagers experience in their peer relationships. More boys than girls talked of loneliness. This may be because boys are less skilled than girls in disclosing personal information, demonstrating affection and support, and avoiding making very negative comments – the very skills which are fundamental to starting and maintaining friendships (Savin-Williams and Berdt 1990).

When the chips are down

We saw in the first half of the chapter that the welfare of friends can lead to positive feelings. Here we see the converse: boys and girls experience negative emotions when things are going badly for their friends:

> I felt sorry for Jan because her boyfriend phoned last night and her dad cut him off the phone. She was dead upset! [f]

> Today I feel like crying because someone said my friend who was killed in a gang fight deserved all he got. I was upset [f]

> I'm worried about two of my friends who've both got involved in drugs [f]

> I feel mad because one of my friends is getting picked on [m]

Bullying

Several boys and girls write about either their own personal experiences of being bullied or instances of others being picked on. Their feelings of distress are palpable:

I feel like killing myself because of the girls at my school. I can't settle in this school. I miss my old friends so I might run away and stay with one of them. I need someone to talk to and get help but I'm too scared. I don't know what to do. I might tan [*slash*] my wrists again but this time I will do a better job [f]

Today will be no different from any other day. I will either get punched or kicked, get called names like 'nae pals', or be just bored all school day long. At lunchtime, if there is a game of football and I start to play, I will be told to 'get lost', and if I don't I will be punched and kicked the whole lunch break [m]

My friend is getting bullied a lot. A lot of boys are calling her names that makes her feel bad about herself. She has told a lot of people, for example parents, youth club leaders and her teacher but nothing much is happening. I feel very sorry about my friend. I wish I could help her more but I've done everything I can [f]

Bullying is a common event in school. People think it's cool to pick on someone. Now I know who my real friends are. You can't really trust anyone, can you? People are changing and so are attitudes. The school tries its best to help but they can't stop people bullying without proof and I don't know where to get it. Perhaps I should try and ignore it as it may go away. What do you think? What do you care anyway? [m]

We saw earlier that some find their experiences of being slagged distressing. Here we see examples of verbal abuse which seem more akin to bullying:

The people in school are calling me names again. I really feel like pulling the plug on my life. I can't cope with it. What really bugs me is that they don't even know me [m]

I would like it if I had nice looks and attracted lots of boys, but when boys walk past me they say look at the ugly bastard. Sometimes I cry myself to sleep at night because I can't stop thinking about it and I want to dog school because I don't want to go in case anyone says anything to me [f]

So much for the adage 'Sticks and stones can break my bones, but names can never hurt me'.

Peer pressure

Peer pressure – or the ability to conform to the behaviours or beliefs of the peer group – are believed to be powerful in adolescence. It may be the price one has pay for being the member of a group (Coleman and Hendry 1990):

I'm dreading another day at school today. My best friend is still absent so I have to face 'them' alone, hang around with 'them' all day. When I say 'them' I mean my 'friends', only they aren't really my friends. I only hang about with 'them' because they're the popular group. I only laugh at their jokes because everyone else does. If I had guts I would stop hanging about with 'them' but I never will because without 'them' I would be nothing. I'm sure others feel the same but would never admit it because, like me, they're scared, scared of 'them'. A large group of popular people can make your life hell and when they slag and tease others I laugh and agree even though inside I feel horrible [f]

My past has been really bad. I had to split with my friends. I went dogging, smoking with them, just because they enjoyed doing it and I was their friend, and had to go with them, and also help them hide their drugs, and give them advice. All I got is 'You are not a person. You are worse than an animal' [f]

I hate people who smoke, drink, etc. because everyone thinks they are trendy and are friends with them. They make you feel really sad (pathetic) and not good enough for them [f]

I hate being pushed about and do not like how everyone thinks that it is cool to smoke or take drugs. If you are not daring or cannot crack a sad joke you are not in the gang, and if you are not in the gang then you get picked on and called names, or people think that they can give you a quick punch or kick every so often and get away with it [m]

Two issues come to mind here. The first, more immediate one, is that peer pressure is powerful and pervasive amongst teenagers. Although we do not see examples here, such peer pressure can be positive too in that it can discourage anti-social behaviour. The second is that not all individuals succumb to these pressures; we know that teenagers differ in their susceptibility to peer pressure, and we have seen examples of individuals exercising independent judgement.

The very length of this chapter reflects the enormous impact that friends and the wider peer group have on the emotional lives of the Howie Feel teenagers. This is particularly marked amongst the girls – an observation which is substantiated throughout Howie Feel. For instance, we saw earlier (in response to the questions 'things which make me happy/unhappy') that friendships emerge as the most salient influence on girls' feelings. Clearly, any consideration of the emotional world of teenagers must acknowledge the powerful influence exercised by their relationships with their peers.

CHAPTER 11

How We Feel About Romance

Early adolescence is a time when young people are becoming sexually aware, consolidating feelings which emerge throughout childhood. Given that there may be potential difficulties in communicating between the sexes at this age (because of embarrassment, etc), experimenting with roles and relationships can be confusing and stressful for teenagers.

From early childhood, adults tease youngsters about having boyfriends or girlfriends. This conveys a message that it is the norm to have such (heterosexual) relationships. Come adolescence, the young person's developing body signals that s/he is ready for a sexual relationship. However, the message from parents now can be different – 'you are not ready to be involved with someone'. Who is it that is not ready? The young person or their parents? Teenage girls, in particular, may receive these mixed messages as it would seem that many parents are more concerned about their daughters entering relationships than their sons.

Of course, not all parents restrict their teenagers in this way and not all teenagers find it difficult to enter into 'romantic relationships'. In fact, relationships with friends allow young people to practise skills and ways of communicating that can carry over into romantic relationships (Sullivan 1953).

These relationships are not always with members of the opposite sex. Although almost all of the information from our survey relates to girl-boy relationships, we cannot assume this means that no young people have sexual feelings for those of the same sex. As it is not unusual for teenagers to have homosexual encounters (albeit short-lived), it is perhaps surprising that in Howie Feel only one boy talks of being gay. This may partly reflect that fact that many teenagers (particularly boys) disapprove of homosexuality – even to the point of being antagonistic towards homosexuals.

We have chosen to use the term 'romance' as part of the chapter heading. The accounts which follow are about relationships with peers that are more than platonic friendships. They are about fancying and being fancied, love, rejection, going out with someone and so on. They are also sometimes about sex and sexual feelings, but not predominantly so. Our term 'romance' has its drawbacks as it is often used in relation to love – not all of the accounts talk of love. We take this phrase, however, to refer to attraction between people which is more than likely to involve physical attraction.

Positive feelings

At the start of the questionnaire quite a large number of young people state that their boyfriends or girlfriends make them happy, with girls more likely than boys to find a relationship a source of happiness. Some of the 'Dear Diary' accounts echo this:

> Today I am feeling really happy as I am going to see Mark at the weekend. As I used to go out with him, at Christmas I am hoping that I might get back to getting off with him [f]

> I wake up in the morning feeling awful. I think why do I have to get up this early in the morning. What gets me alive is saying 'hello' to a very special person (girl) and hoping she will one day be with me. She is nice in every aspect and brings me alive. My life would be complete with her [m]

Interestingly, boys are twice as likely as girls to state that their girlfriends make them feel good *about themselves*. There could be a number of reasons for this. We have seen earlier that girls' friendships are often based on looking out for each other's feelings, comforting each other when times are bad. Boys in general do not seem to have this type of relationship with their friends. Perhaps girlfriends fill this gap for boys, taking care of them and making them feel good about themselves:

> I feel lost and on my own. The only individual I can seek comfort or ease in, is my girlfriend. She is beautiful, kind and caring. I plan to see her tonight [m]

> I felt loved because when I fell out with my friend a girl started to cheer me up. She is a kind hearted girl [m]

For some boys it might be that having a girlfriend gives them status with their peers. Researchers have suggested that this is a common reason for young people entering into relationships (Fine 1977). One 'Dear Diary' account gives us a sense of this, but it is a girl who is enjoying the status:

> I am still over the moon about being with Peter and everybody around me knows it. I have been rubbing people's noses in it and being snide but I don't care. I wouldn't bitch unless I had reason to. Stewart knocked

my bag off my shoulder, I think he's a nice guy – possibly next in line [f]

Fancying and being fancied

Many teenagers talk of fancying someone and being fancied. In our experience of working with teenagers this is an exciting preoccupation, particularly for girls. Howie Feel may surprise us by revealing, in the safety of an anonymous questionnaire, that boys are similarly romantic:

> Today I saw her again…she is so beautiful, I just wish she would notice me now she is my instructor. She is beginning to notice me, I'm top of the shooting class and it's impressing her. Any day now I'm going to ask her out [m]

> I feel so in love with Ewen, I wish he was in every class. I even tried a 'mood-ring' to see what I was like. It came out happy and in love. When I was in Science, which is the class Ewen is in, I couldn't stop staring. Now you know why I am happy [f]

> I am feeling on top of the world because I am going to ask out the guy that I've fancied for ages. But I feel shit cause my friend fancies him too… I think I should go with my feelings. He might even say no and then my friend could be in with a chance [f]

> Today I realised that I'm in love with the girl sitting next to me in my English class. This makes me happy but I don't know if I should tell her, as she might laugh at me. I think I'll tell her one day but until then who knows? [m]

The teenagers talk in a variety of ways about how they feel when they are fancied:

> Today I feel good about myself. I was very chirpy and happy. I was lucky because my friend asked a boy out for me and he said 'yes'! I had fancied him for ages. I got this sick feeling in my stomach which was sickening. I felt on top of the world when he said yes!! [f]

> The boy I fancied chatted to me today! I feel good about that. We're developing a good friendship, I think that's good to start with! [f]

> Today I am feeling quite good about myself because I have been doing my school work quite well and a girl also asked me to go out with her, but I said no because I want to go out with her friend [m]

Happy relationships

Sometimes we, as adults, are guilty of dismissing young relationships as trivial and unimportant. This perhaps stems from the fact that these relationships are very often transient, with the teenagers moving in and out of relationships regularly.

When talking to young people on the subject of relationships, we have found that a relationship can be viewed as anything from one day, a week, months or beyond. However, we should not dismiss the 'here and now' as having no importance. Young people have strong feelings about even short relationships and, for the individual, these feelings don't just feel like 'puppy love':

> I saw my boyfriend and I love him to bits. I hope he loves me too... I can't wait to see him on Friday night, I love him so much [f]

> It was fab this morning before school. Alan phoned and we spoke for a while and then he asked me to go and stay with him, I said 'Yes' now I can't wait. I think I'm in love [f]

For a few girls these feelings extend to long-distance romances:

> I have no problems except one, but it is not really a problem...it's just a stupid little thing about a boy I like and I am not able to see him 'cause he does not stay here...I write to him all the time and that's cool. I talk to him every night on the phone for hours and we have a laugh. That is how I feel so it's good to be here and alive [f]

> The boys in this school seem so immature in comparison to the Greek boys who listened more, appreciated me more and were a lot more romantic [f]

Some talk of the physical side of their relationships. For most, this usually means 'nipping' (kissing):

> I met my girlfriend last night, played football and then snogged her for about 30 minutes, it was good [m]

> On Monday I was asked to nip the same girl who asked me on Saturday. I said no again because I already want to nip someone, but unfortunately she's away to until Friday. She says she will nip me on Friday though and that is why I'm in quite a good mood. I am quite fed up though because I have to wait until Friday... I am going out again tonight and I might just nip someone else while I am waiting for the other girl to come home [m]

Although a few young people make reference to sexual feelings and sexual acts, the numbers are small – so much for those who believe that teenagers are obsessed by sex, drugs and rock and roll. A recent study in Glasgow in fact

Figure 11.1   *Rose Moon*

reveals that the majority of thirteen- and fourteen-year-old teenagers are not having sexual intercourse (Greater Glasgow Health Board 1996).

In Howie Feel it is the boys who are more likely to talk positively about sex – for example, boys are much more likely than girls to say sex is a source of happiness. This gender difference may be due to machismo in some of the boys or it could be that sex is more of an issue for boys at this time. In addition, we have no way of establishing what they mean when they say 'sex'. In the 'Dear Diary' accounts, although the majority of positive accounts about sexual matters are written by boys, this is not exclusively the case:

> I feel really happy as I went quite far with my boyfriend and I really enjoyed it [f]

> My girlfriend is being extraordinarily sexy towards me. Whenever I see her she is always wearing clothes that really turn me on and when I kiss her it feels as if I am on cloud nine [m]

Of course, in our survey we are aware some of the responses will be 'wind-ups'. Sex is one issue which is open for such games, given the sensitive and often taboo nature of sexuality. We have particular difficulty deciding whether accounts which are about sexual fantasies are wind-ups intending to shock. However, as sexual fantasies are the most common sexual activities in which young people engage, we should maybe not be surprised at getting a glimpse of these in some 'Dear Diary' accounts:

> Today I felt on top of the world because my girlfriend let me shag her then I found out that my friend was there and she was on her knees giving him one. Then her friend felt my balls and asked me out and promised me a blow job [m]

Although the explicit nature of adolescents' erotic fantasies do, in part, reflect their burgeoning sexuality, we still have to recognise that Howie Feel may have offered some of the youngsters a very tempting opportunity to indulge in elaborate and anonymous wind-ups.

Notwithstanding, what we witness in Howie Feel is consistent with previous research (e.g. Coles and Stokes 1985) in suggesting that most of the fantasies are about famous celebrities, in particular a certain Pamela Anderson. One boy, however, attempts to engage the reader of the questionnaire:

> If you are a woman reading this and you are nice I would like to… [m]

No thanks pal!

Negative feelings

If having a boyfriend or girlfriend can make a teenager feel confident, attractive and important, then the absence of such a relationship can produce the opposite effects – all of which take their toll on self-esteem.

In 'Dear Diary' we come across a range of negative feelings relating to both not having relationships or being in relationships which are unstable.

Barriers to forming relationships

Throughout the questionnaire many teenagers (particularly girls) feel that they lack confidence. Nowhere is this more evident than in relation to their 'romantic lives':

> There is one girl which I see every day, I do not know how to approach her or talk to her so she takes an interest in me. This is the main depressant in my life [m]

> I also feel I wish I was slimmer and nicer looking because there is a boy I totally love but I know he would not want to go out with me [f]

> I feel insecure towards girls – I feel I have to be perfect to get them to like me [m]

> I am shy about telling certain people how I feel about them, such as how I really like them. I like two certain girls but do not want to let on to them about how strongly I feel about them. I am near them quite a lot and am friends with them, but that is the problem. I am only friends with them. I am scared that if I tell either of them how I feel they might laugh or reject me so I am bottling it all up, keeping it all to myself. Someone else likes one of the girls and I am scared that he will make a move first and I will lose her [m]

> I feel depressed because every time I see Kenny I can't even look at him. On the other hand I am quite happy because at least I saw him. I am feeling kind of proud of myself because at the weekend I was talking to him without my face going red [f]

Rejection

A number of young people in 'Dear Diary' write of their feelings when they are rejected by those they like. How many times, as adults, are we tempted to respond 'there's plenty more fish in the sea'? Reading the accounts, however, we see that such rejection can really hurt:

> Today I asked a girl to go out with me but she said no. I haven't been able to stop thinking about her all day. I couldn't be bothered doing

anything today, I did as little as possible in school and just lay about the house thinking how I would get her to like me and how stupid I was thinking she would like me [m]

Today a girl rejected me at school. I asked her to the cinema and when she said no, I felt so small. I have always liked this girl but I was unable to build up the guts to ask her out and now I am feeling bad [m]

I am sad because I really fancy this boy and he won't go out with me and it really depresses me sometimes [f]

I feel all depressed. A girl I really like got off with me and I was supposed to be going out with her but she's got a boyfriend and she likes him more than me and I think she's going to dump me [m]

Jealousy

Jealousy appears in several guises in Howie Feel. Some teenagers who do not have romantic relationships are jealous of those who do; for others the jealousy is specific to particular individuals:

Today I feel very jealous because a girl I like, likes my best friend better than me. I have thought about giving him a doing but that won't solve anything [m]

I am really jealous of my friends, they all have guys who fancy them and want to get off with them and I don't [f]

I feel very jealous of a girl I know is flirting with the boy I fancy. She always goes up and barges in when I'm talking to him. My friends keep telling me that he does like me and doesn't like the other girl but I'm not so sure [f]

I feel ugly and rejected today as I found out Mr X is going out with the girl with all the clothes, lovely hair, popularity. She makes me want to hit her but I know it is wrong to be jealous [f]

Relationship difficulties

In 'Dear Diary' girls are more likely to talk about being in a romantic relationship than boys. It is possible, in this age group, that girls *are* more likely than boys to be in romantic relationships. Also, as we have seen, girls are more likely than boys to engage with people at an emotional level and, therefore, 'relationships' are perhaps more salient for them; maybe they have more to lose when things don't go well:

I'm going to have to forget a certain boy as I'm going out with another boy. It's going to be a long hard trail of tears, if he ever knew I was writing this he'd probably love the attention [f]

Today I am confused and depressed. I like this person but the problem is he's gone and it is very unlikely that I'll ever see him again. I've tried to talk to my friends but they can't understand. My life is so unfair to me, there is no point in living anymore [f]

In the Field of Words we found that girls are more likely than boys to circle 'confused' and this pattern is echoed here:

There was one boy who really became an enormous part of my life. We spent days, weeks, months together. I was in Heaven. When it ended three weeks ago today I was really upset but it was my decision so why was I upset? I don't know the answer to that question. Even today I still feel very strongly for him but I have grown feelings for another. I am seeing him tonight, the more times I spend with him the more I like him but I can't seem to give up my summer lover. What will happen? I'll wait and see! [f]

Today I feel upset because I asked to nip a boy and he said yes but I don't think he's telling the truth. I think I am in love with him but he asked me if he could shag me, I don't know what to say. I feel very confused [f]

In Howie Feel 'fall outs' are commonly talked about by both sexes, with the difficulties ranging from small 'tiffs' to the breakup of relationships:

I have just fell out with my boyfriend and I feel really numb [f]

I'm fed up. I'm frustrated through a girl... I wish she would talk to me about it so we could sort things out about what is going to happen between the two of us. But if we can't sort it out then I wish for us to be friends and talk to each other when we see each other [m]

My life is ruined because I have split up with my boyfriend for the third time and I really do miss and love him very much and he won't get back with me, but he loves me as well. He said he is sick of girls for the moment [f]

A few of the young people express that they feel under pressure to be in relationships:

I have a great home and a great family but the one thing which annoys me is that I have never entered a relationship with a girl, it feels like a great weight over my shoulders [m]

> Everyone's got a boyfriend but I can't find one [f]

Pressure can also come from within a relationship:

> Last night I had an argument with my boyfriend because I told him we
> were finished but he pressured me into going back out with him and I
> really wished I hadn't went back with him [f]

Just as there are a small number of young people who choose to write about
positive feelings about sex and physical relationships, there are a few who talk
of negative experiences:

> I am really pissed off because I haven't had a bird in ages and I am getting
> mad and I haven't had a shag in ages also, so that is how I feel, really
> pissed off [m]

> I am feeling quite cheery because I lost my virginity a few nights
> ago…but I'm a bit worried because I have skipped a period and am all
> sore and red [f]

> I feel sore, dirty and used. I've missed my period and I'm beginning to
> worry but I'm not sure as I have an uneven cycle [f]

Interestingly, those of us who work with teenagers might make assumptions
that boys are the ones that put pressure on girls to have sex. One account stands
this stereotype on its head:

> I am getting to the age where girls and SEX are coming into my life. So
> far my girlfriend hasn't asked for sex but I'm not sure that it is right for
> us at the present moment [m]

It is, no doubt, easier for girls than boys to admit to feeling pressurised to enter
sexual relationships. It may also be harder for girls to admit they want to have
such relationships. Whether or not young people choose to have sex is, in fact,
partly dependent upon the sexual behaviour of their friends (Cvetkovich and
Grote 1980).

Being slagged about relationships

As we have mentioned earlier, peer influences are important in shaping how
young people feel about themselves and those around them. In relation to
'romance', friends can be a source of support or a source of conflict. Boys may
find themselves being teased unless they conform to the stereotyped 'stud'
image, while girls who enjoy going out with different people are called 'slags'.
This is certainly borne out in some of the 'Dear Diary' accounts:

Figure 11.2   *Emma Guild*

People sometimes tease me because my lack of experience with girls. This does upset me a bit because I do not care what other people think of me [m]

Some of my boyfriend's friends think I am a tart because I go all the way with him [f]

I am getting slagged off for being easy but I'm not [f]

I feel terrible, I am supposed to be going out with someone but I've been flirting with this other boy I really like – some of my friends are turning against me for this as they say I am still all over him [f]

Because young people tend to value the opinion of their friends, their teasing can be hard to bear. One boy, however, feels that it doesn't really matter if his friends disapprove:

I nipped this girl last night and if anyone knew I would get slagged off, but I like the girl and that is all that really matters [m]

These 'Dear Diary' accounts allow us a glimpse into what it is like for some teenagers at a time when young people are forming romantic relationships and experimenting with sex. Given that so much of the research on adolescent sexuality focuses on their sexual *behaviour*, Howie Feel widens the picture by revealing the part played by romantic relationships in their *emotional* lives. Clearly, for many, the dating game results in strong feelings which deserve to be acknowledged and respected.

CHAPTER 12

How We Feel About Everything Else
A Mixed Bag

In 'Dear Diary' the vast majority of our teenagers write about either their emotions in general or focus on the issues covered in earlier chapters (i.e. family life, school, peers). However, some other issues also emerge. By giving young people a 'voice', we are duty bound to reveal *everything* they say, not just the easily classifiable. This leaves us with something of a mixed bag and in this chapter we will reveal its contents.

Action man

In Chapter 2 we revealed that, for boys, the most common response to 'things which make me happy' is participating in sport. Although girls also talk of physical activity in their diary accounts, taking part in sport features again and again in those of the boys:

> The one thing I really like is playing football for my team on Saturday, even if we win or lose, I always enjoy it [m]

> I can't wait till I'm home and go out and play football [m.]

> Today I went to school. The first thing I did was go out to the playground and play football – that made me happy [m]

> I am really looking forward to playing hockey today. I love it! [f]

For some boys their commitment and preoccupation with sport seems to ellipse their entire lives:

> If I didn't have football I wouldn't have a life [m]

> I know it sounds stupid but if girls were not around all that I would do is play football. It is the greatest game ever. When my team get beat I

> won't say I get really depressed and angry. It's such a big part of my life
> that nothing will ever change that [m]

As many physical pusuits provide teenagers with opportunities to be with
others, some value their sociable nature:

> I think PE was very good because we were doing forward rolls and we
> did flips and watched other people doing them and it was very very funny
> in PE [m]

> One of the reasons I feel happy is because I am going to my dancing
> club tonight and we are doing a show very soon and I really have a good
> time when I am at dancing because all my friends which go to my school
> are there and I have a laugh [f]

Some boys and girls value the physical and psychological benefits of sport (we
saw this earlier too in response to 'things which make me feel good about
myself'):

> I love sport because it keeps you fit [f]

> I am also going to play Badminton this evening. I like Wednesdays
> because they are active and when I am being active I feel good [m.]

> Today I don't feel too good. I need a hair cut and need my lunch. Maybe
> a good game of football would help me with my friends [m]

We saw earlier that more boys than girls link 'feeling happy' and 'feeling good
about myself' to winning or achieving at sports. This comes through in their
diary accounts too:

> I'm pleased with myself because I scored a goal in football in PE today.
> I feel strong and confident [m]

> I feel quite healthy today, my October week's holiday has just passed
> when I did a lot of exercise including two rounds of 18 holes of golf at
> _____club. I'm still gloating over my birdie on the 9th! [m]

We see that achieving is not necessarily about winning. Rather, some teenagers
feel good about mastering new skills:

> I got swimming today. I know how to swim now. That feels good. Now
> I'm not the only person who can't swim [f]

> I had a good day today. I learned something new in PE and I felt proud
> of myself because I have not done it before [gender unknown]

Many boys' accounts reveal that they are quite competitive and driven to do
well in sport. Rather than glibly dismissing these accounts as 'just sport', we
should be careful not to lose sight of the fact that any success (whether this

involves winning or mastery of new skills) is likely to be beneficial to their self-esteem.

Where teenagers make negative comments about sport, most concern either performing badly in sport or disliking specific activities:

> I have basketball today and it is not my favourite sport [m]

> Today I feel quite bad because the rugby selectors put me on the bench [m]

> At lunchtime I was getting a bit agitated because I was playing rubbish at badminton [f]

Howie Feel suggests then that, for many, sport is more than a game.

Football crazy

Football seems to be a major preoccupation not only as a physical pusuit but also as a spectator sport (however, all that shouting, groaning and cheering maybe expends a fair bit of energy!). Certainly watching football comes up again and again, with some girls showing themselves to be avid supporters of a particular football team:

> Last night's football result was a good result for me and that has made me feel very pleased today as I love football even though I am a girl [f]

> I feel really annoyed at Rangers training methods. They must be doing something far wrong to get as many injuries as they are getting. XXXXX is an arse-hole. He's done all he can for Rangers and he can't take them any further. He should resign [f]

The sheer volume of boys' references to football, however, swamp those which girls make. In Chapter 2 we saw that nearly one-quarter of boys identify the performance of their favoured football team as sources of happiness or unhappiness. Boys show themselves to be football crazy here too:

> If Rangers win against Juventus I will be happy! [m]

> I feel good today as Celtic's arch rivals were beaten and this always makes me happy [m]

> Rangers got knocked out of the cup last night so I feel angry and bitter [m]

> Well I am quite ashamed today because Rangers got beat last night off Aberdeen 2–1. It would not have been so bad if they had got beat off a better team [m]

Clearly, supporting a football team conjures up a range of emotions. For some supporters there is a feeling of pride or shame – a sense that in some way they are responsible for the result. This is mirrored in the responses of others:

> I am depressed because my favourite football team got beat last night and lots of people are bullying me because of it [m]

> Today I feel really proud because the team I support won last night. I was congratulated by all non-Rangers fans [m]

The fact that football figures so prominently in the accounts is likely to be partly due to the unfortunate timing of Howie Feel Day. Not being football fans, we had not realised that we had scheduled it to run the day after an important game!

Neighbourhood blues

In the diary section many teenagers talk about where they live. For those who choose to do so, their comments are unequivocally negative:

> I stay in a bad area [m]

Most commonly, they complain that in their area they have nothing to do, nowhere to go:

> I feel very tired today. But I feel tired every day, very depressed and bored. All me and my friends do is walk about the streets. There is nothing in _____ for us to do. Sometimes I get very angry about having my own kids and bringing them up in _____. When I get angry I get awful crabit and take everything out on my friends. Everyone thinks I am going daft because of the way I am going but it's not me, it's the place I am living. Today I feel down, I feel as if the world is going round and round and I am going to fall off [f]

> I feel as though there is nothing to look forward to as it is so boring at night. I live in _____ so it is not as though they are going to build a youth club or something because they think it is all drugs there or bad people. If there were more things to do more youngsters would stay out of crime [f]

> I feel under pressure to drink at night because in _____ there is nothing to do except things which you know you shouldn't be doing [f]

> There is nothing to do around my bit. You can either stay in or walk around the streets doing nothing. If you even play football somewhere you get told to go away [m]

Several talk of their clashes with the police:

Figure 12.1   *Cassie Shand*

> When I am out with my friends we have no freedom. We get searched most nights by the police and chased by them for nothing. This is good sometimes but sometimes it is as though we have no freedom [m]

> I love to go out and have a laugh but me and my pals can't even walk along the road without the police booking us – and it is for nothing – I think they are just bored too! [f]

Fears of violence hang over some of the teenagers. We have no way of knowing the extent to which such fears represent real rather than imagined dangers. What is clear is the fact that many young people feel anxious and vulnerable:

> Now when you walk about in my area it is always dodgy in case we meet somebody who will want to batter us or something like that [m]

> It makes me sad that when my Mum sends me to the local shop she can no longer be sure I will return. The amount of violence has increased so greatly I could be murdered or beaten up. Nobody is safe anymore [m]

> In this world today there is a lot of violence and I can not be safe walking the streets so I do not go out. I am depressed [f]

The big (or not so big) three: smoking, alcohol and drugs

It maybe comes as some surprise that in Howie Feel only a few teenagers talk about taking cigarettes, alcohol and drugs. This is consistent with recent research which shows that *regular* use of drugs by this age group in Glasgow is low (Greater Glasgow Health Board 1996).

The Howie Feel accounts suggest that those who do use substances (cigarettes, alcohol and drugs) tend to view their experiences positively:

> I feel good today because I have had a joint and had a bottle of Bucky (*fortified wine*) last night [m]

> I like it when I'm drunk [f]

> I can't wait till Friday and Saturday because that is when I get drunk [f]

Those who talked about drinking often do so with friends or with their boyfriends or girlfriends:

> Today I am very happy, I'll go and get a swally [*drink*] with my friends [m]

> I can't wait til the end of the week to get steamin' and get a boyfriend and get wrecked [f]

Some talk of substances making them feel better:

> I want to go out with my friends and get a drink or smoke because I feel like shit [m]

> I feel depressed and unliked. Sometimes I feel suicidal. It is on a rare occasion when I smile, only when I drink or take stuff [m]

> I don't feel well today. I really need a smoke [m]

> I feel that bad that I feel like dogging school and getting on acid and getting pure steaming [*drunk*] [f]

> ...hash and gas [*butane*] makes you laugh and feel much better... [f]

> I haven't had a bevy [*drink*] for three weeks and maybe I need a pick up...MY LIFE STINKS (except when I'm allowed out with my friends for a bevy [f]

As the following accounts illustrate, some argue that their substance use fulfils a supportive function, acting as a sort of coping strategy.

> I've already slashed my wrists, it didn't work. I'm still alive. I wish I wasn't. I wish I was still in my Children's Home near my family...I have not had a drink for a long time but I feel it's the only thing I can turn to [f]

> I'd probably kill myself if I had the guts but instead I just go out and get drunk. It's the best solution. No one understands me [f]

Although the numbers talking about substance use are small, we do nonetheless get a glimpse into the reasons they offer for their activity.

Wet wet wet

As a nation we are obsessed by the weather. Predictably then, references to the weather crop up a lot in teenagers' accounts. Presumably, one of the reasons why the weather is such a popular topic of conversation is because it affects the way we feel. In fact, about 6 per cent of our teenagers say that the weather makes them feel unhappy. This preoccupation with climatic conditions spills into the diaries. We could fill pages and pages with their weather talk, but we have just included a few:

> We had a great laugh at lunchtime getting wet in the rain [gender unknown]

> I'm pretty depressed at the bad weather [m]

Went to the window and saw the rain, got immediately depressed. It's been like this, the rain always gets me down [m]

The weather was thunder and lightning so it made me feel excited and anxious [f]

We can assure you that the West of Scotland isn't *always* wet.

Money matters

Although in earlier sections of the questionnaire we saw that quite a few teenagers feel that money (or lack of) contributes to their happiness or unhappiness, only a small number write about their financial situation in the diary section:

I wish I had more money because I want to buy my Dad and sister decent birthday presents [m]

I am feeling down today because I don't have any money and my friends have all gone into town and I can't because I don't have a job and that's why I don't have any money [f]

Life is just so boring just now. I can't get a job, I can't get money and there is nothing to do for free [f]

In the main then, young people seem to regard money as their passport to 'doing something'.

High days and holidays

As we would expect, teenagers express positive feelings about events such as birthdays:

It was my birthday five days ago and I got a lot of nice presents. My birthday proved to me how much people care about me because everyone in my family and a lot of my friends came to visit me or phoned to wish me a happy birthday [f]

Today is my birthday so I'm quite happy and on top of the world [f]

Some talk about Christmas, although two months away:

I just can't wait until Xmas [f]

Although I feel quite bad I still can't wait till Guy Fawkes night, my birthday and Xmas. I would love to spend Xmas with my family [m]

I'm quite happy and excited about Xmas because it is getting dark earlier. This feels good but I'm worried about a money source for Xmas gifts [gender unknown]

A handful talk about looking forward to going on holiday:

I can't wait until the holidays and I'm going to Paris next year so that should be good fun. No parents and only a few teachers. Ahh, bliss! [f]

Racism

When we developed the questionnaires we were very keen to be able to identify the feelings of teenagers from ethnic minority groups. However, after debating the issue, we decided that it would be insensitive to ask teenagers to indicate their race on their questionnaires. We therefore lost the opportunity to comment on the particular issues of ethnic minority groups. We can only isolate one account which provides us with such a picture:

It is hard being me today as I am a black man living in a white man's country. I am involved in a lot of gang violence and there are many people who want to kill or at least slash me. My parents do not like it if I go out late at night as they are scared that I may not return. I know this but I want to prove to the people who want to kill me that even though they have given me a death threat, I am not scared of them…I am scared of no-one as I can get over 500 people to kick them in. The police never stop the white people if there is a fight between the whites and the blacks. I myself have been stopped many times by the police for no reason. I do not think that anyone would like to be me but I like it and in a few years I will be moving back home with a few of my friends so I will be OK [m]

Current affairs

Several teenagers fill the 'Dear Diary' section with their comments about the goings on in the wider world. Such concerns are wide ranging:

I am upset by the fact that Marti Pellow is going to marry [f]

Take That are meant to be splitting up at Christmas, I am really upset and just wish I could curl up and die [f]

I got up quite early this morning, watched the news. The wars are still going on and people are still getting killed [f]

Life on earth could be better if there weren't any wars or pollution [f]

I think the crap produced by television companies are giving today's youth the wrong impression. They are saying that it is OK to be homosexual, fornicate, swear, smoke, drink, take drugs. This is the cause of our youth having mental health problems. I think the Health Board should shut down the soaps that are polluting the minds of our youth [m]

I think the government should do more things about teenagers smoking and drinking and under age sex and try to prevent these [f]

Reading some of the teenagers' accounts we can't help but wonder whose attitudes and values we are seeing. From the literature we know that, contrary to popular wisdom, teenagers are likely to grow up holding rather than rejecting the values held by their parents. Is this what we are seeing here? Do some of the accounts reflect what teenagers are hearing at home?

Pets' corner

Whereas younger children tend to be quite fixated on their pets, very few of our teenagers' accounts touch on this:

I went to the bathroom where on the way my friendly dog ran over to see me. I love my dog very much [m]

Just over a year ago my dog died. When I think about him it makes me feel very sad. As much as I want to, I try very hard not to think about him [m]

Health matters

In Chapter 6 we saw that many teenagers talk of the way they feel *physically*, for instance saying that they feel tired. We find that many also talk of their general health, which is maybe not surprising especially when we recognise the inter-relationship between the body and the mind. We should bear in mind that stress can manifest itself in many ways, including tension headaches, tummy cramps and upsets, nausea and various muscular aches and pains:

Today I feel very nauseous. I don't feel well. I feel cramped and claustrophobic. I feel sick [m]

Today has been okay so far except for the fact that I have a splitting headache. Headaches suck [m]

Violent thoughts, violent actions?

We have already looked at some of the violent thoughts and actions of teenagers in relation to particular people (e.g. peers) or issues (e.g. racism). In addition to these, a small number of individuals express violent thoughts which fall out with the categories which we have covered so far:

> I still get the dreams of revenge, though not as much as I used to. I'm still going to get them one of these days [m]

> I feel as if I want to get extremely drunk and then beat up the person that killed my brother. Then I would feel better. I want to go out to lunch and eat fast foods. I feel fed up, confused, angry, brave, frustrated and annoyed with God. I want to go out and enjoy myself with my mates, spend lots of money, be generous and go out with some girls. I want to beat up another few people and I want to be very cheeky to someone in authority [m]

> I wish I could hit somebody with a black widow [m]

We are, of course, unable to tell which (if any) of the above comments represent genuine intentions and which have no meaning beyond the level of thoughts or fantasies. Either way, we're left to wonder where these disturbing thoughts come from.

Wind-ups

A very small number of the inevitable wind-ups provided us with a lot of amusement. Thanks guys:

> I feel like chicken tonight [m]

– funny the first time but by the time the sixth boy wrote this, the joke paled somewhat.

> My hamster has fallen out with me because I said he had big teeth [m]

> I saw a ghost last night

> P.S. I really did.

> P.P.S You calling me a liar. Don't get wide [m]

And then, of course, there were the very elaborate and imaginatively detailed accounts of the sexual exploits by some of the boys. These would sit more comfortably within a Nancy Friday book of sexual fantasies. As we want to hold onto our jobs, we will keep these under lock and key – for the moment at least!

CHAPTER 13

Taking Howie Feel On Board
What Can We Do?

Let's take stock now. In Howie Feel we have heard of the personal internal lives of young people in their mid-adolescent years. Their voices combine to create a rich and intricate tapestry – full of friends, family, romance, school and even (wet) weather. What is new in this research is the fact that we have been privileged to hear young people reflect on these aspects of their lives *on their own terms* – to say what is important for them. In fact, the common thread running throughout this tapestry is one of feelings – some of which are intensely personal. It follows that any understanding of young people must acknowledge how they *feel*.

Clearly young people are not homogeneous. The challenge for us then is how to respond to their sometimes disparate needs. How do we do this? What about *our* emotions and the way *we* feel? How do we reconcile the two? A starting point must surely be mutual respect – an acknowledgement that how we feel matters.

Just as we must continue to learn from young people, we can also learn from each other. In our book we have asked various people who work with adolescents to share their experiences with us. We hope that this will enable us to move to a fuller and more sophisticated understanding of how we can all play a part in promoting the mental health of the teenagers we care about.

Howie Feel is about giving young people a voice. This task is worthless unless these voices are heard. It is time now to hear from those who are in the business of *listening* to young people.

CHAPTER 14

Giving Young People a Voice

Jenny Secker

Introduction

At the same time as Jacki and Gillian were carrying out the Howie Feel research in Glasgow, the Health Education Board for Scotland (HEBS) commissioned a study to explore younger children's views about their emotional needs (Hill *et al.* 1996b). Taken together, the two studies provide valuable information about what is important to children and young people from five to fifteen years of age. In doing so, they increase our understanding of how we can support children as they grow up and give them the best chance of becoming secure, happy adults.

This chapter begins by looking at why children's views about their emotional health and well-being are important. I will then look at some of the similarities and differences between the HEBS research and the Howie Feel study and draw out what we can learn from the two studies.

Why do children's views matter?

Most people would probably agree that the advances made in medical science are amongst the greatest achievements of the past fifty years. A great deal is now known about the causes of ill-health and ways of treating it and we all benefit from this increase in knowledge. However, just as many medical treatments have side effects with which we have to cope, this increase in knowledge has had its own side effects. In particular, as medical and psycho-

---

Dr Jenny Secker was formerly the Specialist Research and Evaluation Officer (Mental Health and Special Needs) for the Health Education Board for Scotland and is now a Senior Research Fellow at the Centre for Mental Health Services Development, King's College, London.

logical knowledge has grown, we have become increasingly dependent on doctors and other professionals to help us in times of ill-health and to advise us about looking after our health. In turn, this means that professional views about what it means to be ill or healthy have come to dominate. Clearly, these views are valuable and important, but they are only one way of looking at health and ill-health.

As we grow up and gain experience of our bodies and our emotions, we develop our own understandings of them and these may be different from the professional view. For example, although we know that smoking is one of the worst things we can do for our health, Hilary Graham's research has shown how, for some women, a cigarette provides a much needed release from the pressures of daily life and might even therefore be viewed as 'healthy' in the sense of enhancing the quality, if not the quantity, of life (Graham 1994). Such different views make it important for doctors and other professionals to give us clear explanations of what they are doing and why, but it is also important for them to understand our views too – if they don't, they may not be able to find ways of helping us look after our health which make sense to us and which we are therefore happy to put into practice.

Because people's own ideas about health and ill-health are so important, researchers like Hilary Graham have been exploring the views of adults for some time. However, much less attention has been paid to children's views. One reason for this is that children have traditionally been seen only as adults in the making rather than as people in their own right, with their own feelings and views which make sense to them. In recent years, though, these ideas have started to change. We now recognise that children have the right to information and choices about issues that affect their lives and this has led to legal changes such as the Children Act, which places emphasis on children's and young people's views. We may not agree with all the changes some professionals would like to see but the discussion and debate surrounding child care and children's rights help us to question our assumptions and to recognise that children are not just undeveloped adults.

In keeping with these changing ideas, a few studies have now explored children's views about health, but these have tended to focus on physical rather than mental and emotional health issues. Mental and emotional health is, however, of crucial importance for children's development. In the first place, it is well recognised that childhood experiences can have a profound effect on our mental health as adults. For example, if children are not helped to understand and come to terms with the death of a close family member, they may be left feeling that somehow it is their fault and the guilt they carry as a result may affect their confidence and self-esteem as adults.

However, children's mental and emotional health is not important simply because children are the adults of the future. Mental and emotional problems are far more common amongst children and young people than even GPs often recognise. There is, therefore, an urgent need to find ways of ensuring that children enjoy as secure and happy a childhood and adolescence as possible. Understanding their views of mental and emotional health is a vital part of this and it was with this aim that both the HEBS study and the Howie Feel research were undertaken.

In both studies, finding ways to enable children and young people to express their views was essential. The Howie Feel researchers have already described how they achieved this by using a questionnaire with open questions and plenty of space for young people's own words. For the HEBS study, Professor Hill and his colleagues at Glasgow University developed a range of techniques such as brainstorming, visual prompts and role plays. Using these techniques, they interviewed a total of 96 children aged five to twelve in small groups of about six children, while a further 28 children were interviewed individually. At the end of each interview the children filled in a short questionnaire, which included space for their own drawing. Even the youngest children who took part in the study were able to explain their feelings to the researchers and the interviews produced much valuable information. In the rest of this chapter the children's views are compared with those of the Howie Feel sample.

Similar but different: The concerns of children and young people

One of the striking things about the HEBS and Howie Feel studies is the similarity between many of the themes which emerge. It appears that the concerns of children and young people aged five to fifteen revolve, to a large extent, around similar issues. Naturally, there are some issues which are of little concern to younger children but which are very important in adolescence, such as boyfriends and girlfriends and, for girls especially, physical appearance. In addition, there are some aspects of life which are of peripheral concern to younger children, but which become centrally important as they grow up. In particular, school life does not appear to be a major source of happiness or upset for the younger children, except in relation to friendship and peer group issues. However, some of the older children in the HEBS study begin to express the kind of worries about doing well at school which are a main source of anxiety for the young people who contributed to Howie Feel.

A further difference concerns children's views about their safety. For the youngest children in the HEBS study, fears about safety revolve not around the issues adults worry about, such as strangers and road accidents, but around issues like nightmares and ghosts, which adults might see as less 'real'. These fears recede with age but, even amongst the older children, they are not replaced by concerns about personal safety. In contrast, the young people in the Howie

Feel study express considerable concerns about safety, which are mainly related to violence in the streets.

Clearly, these differences reflect children's changing experiences and needs at different stages of their development, as well as the growing demands of the world around them. However, it would be wrong to suggest that there is a point where these changes suddenly take place. Rather, the HEBS and Howie Feel studies suggest that in many areas of life there is a gradual change of emphasis as children grow up. Where relevant, these developmental shifts are examined in the following discussion of two aspects of life which are of concern to all the children and young people who took part in the two studies: family life and relationships with friends and other peers.

Family life

Unsurprisingly, for the great majority of children and young people the love and security provided by their immediate family, and especially their parents, is of central importance. Amongst the younger children in the HEBS study this appears to be so central that it is almost taken for granted. These children rarely identify parents as a source of happiness, but their experiences of love and security emerge strongly from their descriptions of the reassurance and help provided by their parents. As children grow up, though, they appear to become more conscious of, and more explicitly grateful for, their parents' love and concern, so that a high proportion of the Howie Feel sample identify their family as an important source of happiness.

Alongside this emerging consciousness of the value of family life, however, children's perceptions of their parents' role in providing security and protection also begin to shift, particularly where discipline is concerned. Although some of the youngest children in the HEBS study do identify 'getting a row' or 'being grounded' as a source of unhappiness, the older ones in the study appear to accept the need for discipline of this kind, unless they feel that some unfairness is involved. For those young people who contributed to Howie Feel, though, 'being grounded' and other forms of discipline, such as constraints on where they go and what time they come home, are a source of considerable tension with their parents. For these young people, discipline is no longer a relatively simple matter of 'fair' or 'unfair' punishment but an ever-present illustration of the tension between their own increasing need for independence and their parents' concern to provide an appropriate degree of protection. As one girl puts it:

> At the moment I would love to run away and get away from everything. I want to escape from my parents telling me what to do and constantly trying to rule my life. I hate them. It's as if my Mum doesn't want me to

have any fun. She says she knows what it is like to be 14 but I don't think she does, she couldn't possibly (Howie Feel)

In contrast, although the children in the HEBS study are concerned that their wishes are taken into account, in the main they accept the limits placed on them by parents and don't seek greater freedom. It has to be remembered, though, that the young people who contributed to Howie Feel also describe many positive aspects of their changing relationship with their parents. For one girl, for example, this means a more equal, adult relationship: 'My Mum and I are like good friends' (Howie Feel).

While the concerns generated by children's growing need for independence emerge strongly only in adolescence, concerns about other aspects of family life appear to be important regardless of age. In particular, harmonious family relationships, especially between parents, are identified by both the children in the HEBS study and the Howie Feel sample as a source of happiness. Conversely, arguments between parents are of great concern to both groups – not least because even the youngest children are aware that these can be a sign of parents splitting up. These extracts from the two studies show how central these concerns are throughout childhood and adolescence:

> I've got this funny feeling and I think it's going to come true one day, when my Mum and Dad had a huge argument one day, and my Mum said to my Dad, if you're not happy you know what you can do, and I was upset because after that I always had a feeling that my Dad was going to go away (HEBS study)

> Today I feel a bit better than I did yesterday. I was feeling sad because my parents fell out, although they are not back to normal yet they are gradually talking more and more (Howie Feel)

Before leaving the subject of family life it is important to mention the significance of brothers and sisters and other of family members. As these extracts illustrate, the former can be a source of both happiness and upset across all ages:

> I want to be a paediatrician when I'm older…cause I like handling babies and children, I've got a wee brother and a wee sister…and I've got hundreds of step brothers and sisters (HEBS study)

> Everything's good at home and me, my sister and brother are all close and I'm getting on really well with my sister's boyfriend (Howie Feel)

> I fight with my sister, she gets attention from my parents and I feel left out (HEBS study)

> My sister's really annoying me and I hate it. I never get any time or peace to do any homework or study (Howie Feel)

Where other family members are concerned, a major cause of upset for many of the children and young people who took part in the two studies is the death of a grandparent or other close relative. Parents may, therefore, be faced with the need to comfort their children at a time when they themselves are grieving for the death of their own parent. As will be seen in the next section, despite their resentment at times, on the whole children and young people feel their parents meet these challenges well. First though, the issue of relationships with friends and other peers needs to be discussed because this is also extremely important to the children and young people.

Friendship, falling out and fighting

The importance of family life to children and young people is unlikely to be surprising to anyone reading this book. However, some adults may not realise how important friendship and relationships with other peers can be, even to very young children. In the HEBS study, as with Howie Feel, friends are identified as a main source of happiness, again especially by girls, for example:

> When my best friend was on holiday once...for around 30 days...and then another 30 days...cause it was over school days she was away too, and then she came back and it was probably the happiest I've ever been, because when I saw her and it was like tears came to my eyes, because it was happy tears (HEBS study)

Precisely because friends are so important, they can also be a source of real sadness and pain. Just as a large proportion of the Howie Feel sample identify friendship difficulties as amongst the main things that make them unhappy, so this is a major theme of the HEBS study. These two extracts show how similar issues are of great concern across the age groups:

> Me and Ruby, we've got two friends, Katy and Susan, and they're best friends, and me and Ruby are best friends, and I get upset when Ruby goes off with the other friends...and Katy, I don't know why she does it...but sometimes she tries to drive you away from your other friend and Katy and Ruby say (to each other) 'Can you be my best friend?'... So they came and told me and I was very upset (HEBS study)

> I wonder how it's going to be today between me and my best friend and this other girl who's kind of her best friend, but she says she's my friend too. I feel like there's always some stupid competition between me and this other girl which is just so annoying. She always copies her and agrees with any thing she says just to get her attention (Howie Feel)

Although one boy in the HEBS study does describe a painful experience of being let down by a friend, for the most part the boys appear to experience fallings out and arguments less intensely. As one boy suggested, while girls' fallings out are expressed in the kind of feuds illustrated above, boys seem more likely simply to fight it out:

> When it's the girls that are fighting, their fighting is arguments, but when the boys are fighting, we're always kicking people everywhere and that and punching and everything, aren't we Peter? (HEBS study)

These differences between young boys and girls in the quality and intensity of their friendships and fallings out reflect almost exactly the greater emphasis placed on the same issue by the girls who contributed to Howie Feel. For many of the children and young people in both studies, however, when arguments and fighting take place, not in the context of friendships and fallings out but of malicious teasing and bullying, this is a cause of great unhappiness and pain. These extracts show how upsetting such destructive peer relationships can be to children of all ages:

> And a few, you know, it's like when one of my friends were not – maybe it's trainers that's not a brand make, you know, or something, they get teased and everything. And they tend to tease you and say you're so immature, you're babies and things (HEBS study)

> It feels OK to be me today because I'm not slagged. I have decent clothes and trainers so no-one can laugh at me (Howie Feel)

> There was one boy in our school, and he just like, he went about picking fights with people he knew he could beat, and I stepped in. He started fighting with someone and I stepped in and stopped him, and then he's got big heels, and he ripped all down my face and I was angry at that (HEBS study)

> Today will be no different from any other day. I will either get punched or kicked, get called names like 'nae pals', or just be bored all school day long (Howie Feel)

Clearly, both childhood and adolescence can be a painful as well as a happy time. The following section looks at children's and young people's views about how best adults can help them with the concerns they describe.

How can we support children and young people?

One of the most heartening things about the HEBS and Howie Feel studies is the confidence the children and young people express in adults, and especially in their parents. It is particularly reassuring that amongst the children who took part in the HEBS study, the great majority clearly feel happy and secure most of the time. Similarly, although the young people who contributed to Howie Feel are not slow to express their resentment about what they perceive to be unnecessary restrictions on their independence, many of them also make it clear that feelings of happiness, security and confidence are just as strong. From the children's and young people's own accounts, much of the credit for this is due to their parents. In both studies, parents, especially mothers, are identified as the easiest people to talk to and the most helpful at times of upset or anxiety. Other family members, particularly grandparents, brothers and sisters are also often identified as helpful and supportive. Teachers, though less important as confidants, are regarded by children in the HEBS study as people who can be of real help in some situations.

One of the main ways in which the children and young people say parents and other adults help them to feel happy and secure is to make sure they know they are loved and valued. In the HEBS study, feeling important is a very common theme. Unsurprisingly, for the younger children this is often associated with treats or being the centre of attention, for example on birthdays. For the older children and for the Howie Feel sample, however, feeling important is increasingly associated with being praised for efforts and achievements, and with recognition of their increasing maturity. As one girl explains: 'The most important I've ever felt is like when I get treated like a grown up, and treated like I'm capable of doing things...and that happens quite a lot' (HEBS study).

It follows from this that, as adults, we need to be aware that younger children can experience real distress when they feel we have let them down, perhaps by forgetting a promised treat or postponing an outing. From their point of view, it is not just that the treat or outing hasn't materialised; their distress also comes from their feeling that they are not important to us, at least at the time. Equally, with older children and young people we need to recognise efforts and achievements, but we also need to realise that criticism can be very hurtful. We can probably all think of times when we've been hurt in this way ourselves and these extracts from the Howie Feel study show how distressing this can be to young people too:

> School seems to be getting more and more confusing and boring. My teacher said I was a failure because I didn't understand.

> My Mum sometimes criticises me and makes me feel as if she can't accept me for who I am.

When children and young people feel valued and loved, they also feel more able to deal with the ups and downs of life. However, knowing how to respond at times of upset and worry is also important. One of the clearest messages to emerge from the HEBS and Howie Feel studies is that we need to be better than we sometimes are at being aware of how children and young people feel, at listening to what they say and at understanding how important things that may seem trivial to us are to them. As this extract from one of the HEBS group interviews shows, even quite young children are well aware when adults are not really listening to them or offer false reassurance without taking the time to understand:

> Parents are all saying 'Don't worry' they never say anything else. They just say 'Don't worry', they never help you / It's only words. It's not feelings, it's only words / It's not helping you, it's just, like what they think but it doesn't.

Similarly, many of the Howie Feel sample say they would like their parents to listen to them when they are unhappy, for example:

> I want my Mum to understand how I feel about things.

> I wish my Mum and Dad would listen to me and not keep having arguments with me and blaming me for everything.

Clearly, then, listening and trying to understand are the first responses children and young people need when they are upset or worried. As many of the children who took part in the HEBS study recognise this is not always easy when we are busy or worried ourselves. It might make it easier, though, to realise that being listened to is often all that is needed and that taking time to listen may well prevent a worry from growing into a major upset. If they feel their concerns are understood, children will often be able to cope with whatever is troubling them themselves. For example, when girls, in particular, are distressed by friendship difficulties, they usually don't want adults to intervene, but they do want their distress to be taken seriously. From their point of view, friendship difficulties are no less painful than the relationship difficulties adults experience, and most of us wouldn't dream of responding to an adult in that situation simply by saying 'Don't worry' or 'Find someone else.'

At other times, however, children and young people do want us to intervene. For younger children, the simple steps we usually take quite naturally to 'make it better' are very effective. This might mean a special treat or something to distract them from the upset, or most often it might mean a reassuring cuddle. Up to the age of at least nine or ten, children say they very much appreciate physical comfort from the adults they feel close to.

For older children and young people, practical action can also be important – and this is particularly true where verbal harassment and bullying are concerned. Many schools now have policies to deal with physical bullying and parents can play their part by ensuring that these are in place and working effectively. However, adults don't always realise that verbal harassment, like cruel teasing and name calling, can also be extremely distressing. It is clear from both the HEBS and Howie Feel studies that more action on this by both schools and parents would be greatly appreciated and would address some of the issues that worry children and young people most.

Working out when to take action and when to support children to sort things out themselves can be something of a balancing act, especially as they grow up and need greater independence. As several of the children in the HEBS study tell us though, simply asking what a child wants us to do is often the best way of finding out. It may help, too, realise that as children grow up the support and help of friends becomes increasingly important. Although adult support continues to be highly valued, one in two of the Howie Feel sample, and many of the older children in the HEBS study, also identify their friends as people they can talk to about their feelings. Being able to seek help from friends and being able to offer it are good resources for adult life and these extracts from the two studies show how even quite young children can develop the skills to do both:

> Children can help each other [*with friendship difficulties*] though. Adults can't do that because they don't know what they're feeling. (HEBS study)

> If it wasn't for my friends, I wouldn't be coping so well. I always want to be with them and talk to them. I don't know where I would be without them. (Howie Feel)

> Most people in our class care about Gary because em I think he's got a slight problem and Tim always bullies him... If he was crying, they would say, are you all right and stuff. Come with me and keep away from Tim. (HEBS study)

> My friends usually come to me with their problems. That makes me feel good. (Howie Feel)

As adults, one of the ways in which we can help children grow up feeling happy and secure is, therefore, to recognise the importance of their friendships and to support them in helping each other by providing the love and understanding they need to be able to do so.

Conclusion

What are the main lessons we can learn from the HEBS and Howie Feel studies? First, we can take a great deal of reassurance from the fact that the children and young people who took part in the studies value and appreciate the love and support we already give them. We can also derive reassurance from the fact that the steps we take to offer practical help are felt by children and young people to be effective. So, 'more of the same' is the first answer to the question. Verbal harassment is one issue, however, with which children and young people would like more practical assistance; so we probably need to understand a little better than we do how distressing this is and take steps to address it.

Overall though, the children and young people who took part in the studies are not looking for major changes in what adults *do* to support them. What they would like to see is a change in our *attitudes* to them. They would like us to attend more closely to their concerns, realise that things that may seem trivial to us are painful and distressing for them and, above all, they want us to listen and understand. As one group of children who took part in the HEBS study puts it, we need to:

STOP – and think about children's point of view

LOOK – for their feelings

LISTEN – to what they say.

These are simple things if we can make the time to do them, but they will go a long way to ensuring that children grow up feeling happy and secure.

CHAPTER 15

Young People in Crisis

Anne Houston

Introduction

ChildLine is an organisation dedicated to helping children and enabling their voices to be heard. It provides a free, confidential telephone counselling service for any child or young person with any problem throughout the UK. Since its launch in 1990, ChildLine Scotland has been answering calls from children here. My aim in this chapter is to attempt to set the Howie Feel findings into a wider context, based on the experience of what children and young people tell us at ChildLine Scotland.

There are some obvious similarities in the concerns for young people who call ChildLine Scotland and for those completing the Howie Feel questionnaire – namely family relationships, bullying and the importance of friendships and relationships generally. There is a great emphasis in Howie Feel on school, school work and doing well. Whilst these concerns are not among the problems raised most commonly on our telephone lines, young people do call us about these pressures (Hall 1996).

Young people tend to call ChildLine when they are in particular distress: calls to ChildLine Scotland are more often about pregnancy, sexual and physical abuse, the facts of life and sexuality issues, although no problem is considered too small. In contrast to this, the Howie Feel survey reflects the concerns of young people *generally* rather than those who would identify themselves as at a point of crisis and in need of confidential help. There are, however, a small number of individuals in Howie Feel who seem to be experiencing high levels of distress relating to these specific problems. There are also references to contributory concerns – for example a large number of young people in Howie

---

Anne Houston is the Director of ChildLine Scotland.

Feel talk of the importance of appearance and clothes. These anxieties also feature in calls to ChildLine.

I would like now to look more closely at the nature of the feelings expressed by callers to ChildLine and those taking part in the Howie Feel survey.

Emotions

Howie Feel research demonstrates a clear association between feeling happy and feeling confident. Conversely, others talk of feeling unconfident, particularly in relation to being depressed and lonely. This relates strongly to what we hear at ChildLine. Confidence and self-esteem are often lacking in young people who call us. Whereas ChildLine is in contact with those teenagers who are struggling with their problems, it was a pleasure for me to read also of the positive emotions experienced by young people in Howie.

However, the sense of confusion which runs through many of the Howie Feel accounts is familiar to us at ChildLine: 'I feel worthless sometimes, and I feel unsure about my future...I put on an act that I am fine and cheerful but deep down I am confused and upset about different things.'

Young people regularly talk to us about their attempts to disguise their emotions and feelings and this is often associated with not wanting to burden others – usually parents.

School

School can be seen as a positive experience or a source of insecurity and anxiety, often depending on what else is happening in a young person's life at the time. Both the experience of ChildLine Scotland and the results from Howie Feel reveal bullying to be a major concern for young people. In fact, bullying is now one of the most commonly identified problems for callers to ChildLine Scotland with over 2300 young people talking to our counsellors on this subject last year. ChildLine hears descriptions covering the whole range of bullying behaviours, from name calling, isolation and extortion through to being physically attacked. Bullying experiences, including 'being slagged' (ridiculed) and being cut out of friendships, also feature in Howie Feel. The levels of distress expressed are often high: 'The people in school are calling me names again. I really feel like pulling the plug on my life. I can't cope with it.'

Many young people attach major importance to not 'being different', whether in appearance, clothing or behaviour. To be different leaves a young person open to being bullied.

ChildLine has learned a great deal about the problem of bullying, from the bullied young person, the bystander and, at times, the bully. It is clear that this subject deserves continued attention from education departments, schools, parents and those who care for children generally.

Young people who are being bullied need love, comfort and support, and ways need to be found to increase their self-esteem and self-confidence. Following our recent study *Why Me? Children talking to ChildLine about Bullying* (MacLeod and Morris 1996), we recommend that concerned adults should take the following steps to help a child or young person who they suspect to be the victim of bullying:

1. To stop and listen to what the young person is saying and to check out with them if your understanding, as an adult, is the same as theirs. This may take a few minutes or may take several hours/sessions over a period of time.

2. To allow the young person time and space to describe their anxieties and fears about the results of telling and not telling and also the likely consequences of any planned action.

3. To ask the young person for their suggestions about what can be done and to agree with them a joint plan of action.

Howie Feel echoes our experience that young people can become extremely anxious or depressed about exams and associated pressures to do well. In fact, numbers of such calls to ChildLine peak immediately prior to the major examinations taking place. Young people also talk about the pressure they feel to meet others', particularly parents', expectations of them and their fears about future employment prospects: 'I feel depressed because want to have a good job and a good future to support my family. I am scared in case I won't get a good job'.

Problems or difficulties experienced in the build-up to the exams can be exacerbated if there are other difficulties at home, either between the parents or between the parents and the young person themselves.

Family

The importance of family relationships feature highly in both Howie Feel and ChildLine Scotland information. Some parents assume that young people phone ChildLine with a litany of complaints about them. It is much more complex than this and often young people tell us that they know their parents only want the best for them: 'My parents can be a pain sometimes, and overprotective, but that's only because they love me and I love them'.

As young people try to make sense of the range of their feelings and needs, they rarely put all the blame in one place. Rather than looking to blame anyone, they may just need the opportunity to talk and think through what is going on. Negotiation is the key throughout this period but can be difficult to achieve.

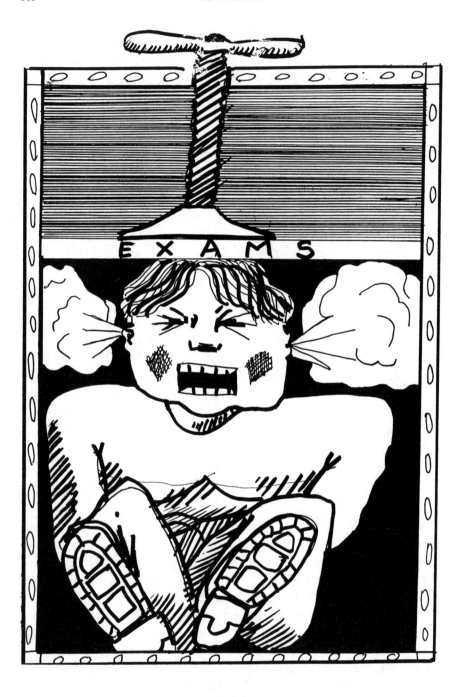

Figure 15.1   Jillian Murphy

Nowadays, many teenagers will have experienced the separation of their parents. The things young people say in Howie Feel about being part of a family that has split up are extremely similar to what we hear every day at ChildLine: 'I wish my parents were still married and loved each other'. They express a desire for magical solutions in a kind of fantasy of wanting 'everything to be better.' They may also feel torn between parents, with divided loyalties. We hear of young people being asked to choose between parents and finding this impossible. They need to talk to someone who is not directly involved, someone who can be objective. There may also be implications for other aspects of their life: 'I feel rejected by my father and boys in general, I wish my Dad would phone'.

So far I have highlighted some of the difficulties young people can have in relation to their families. However, family members are often the first people that would be looked to in a time of upset. They can be seen as major supports and extremely important: 'as long as I have friends and family I will stay confident and strong'.

Friends

The importance of friends comes out again and again both in calls to ChildLine and in the Howie Feel material. Friends can have a very positive influence acting as a sounding board or confidant. They are important at this stage in a young person's development and perceived to be as important as the family in many ways. It is with friends that young people share their hopes and fears and spend large amounts of time. If there are difficulties at school, seeing friends there can make it bearable.

Howie Feel research shows that young people feel good if they are able to help their friends as well as when they themselves are helped. This confirms what young callers to our lines tell us. More than one in ten of the calls to ChildLine Scotland are from someone worried about, and trying to help, a friend. Young people may want to check out that what they are trying to do 'is right' or they may sometimes feel burdened with the information they have been asked to carry. They want to be able to talk it through without breaking a confidence and then return and be there again for their pal. ChildLine's research has also shown that young people may confide in a friend about physical or sexual abuse where they would not contemplate telling an adult. Friends are also often trusted confidants when a young person is being bullied.

Sometimes, as adults, we can be quick to see friends as a 'bad influence' – indeed, at times they may be. However, we also need to be prepared to recognise the positive side of peer relationships.

Boyfriends and girlfriends

'Romantic' relationships, or lack of them, can help or hinder confidence levels for young people in the age group targeted in Howie Feel. Such confidence can very quickly be boosted or can be swept away:

> I feel brilliant today because the boy I fancy has noticed me today.

> The one thing which annoys me is that I've never entered a relationship with a girl. It feels like a great weight over my shoulders.

We get many calls from teenagers in this age group about sex related matters and fears about possible or actual pregnancy. We have been quite surprised and concerned by the lack of knowledge and understanding of sex education.

Gender differences

Around four times as many girls call ChildLine compared with boys. In Howie Feel this is, perhaps, reflected in boys' comments and what they say they want to happen if they feel bad. More of the boys say they would want 'to be left alone' and express a view that they ought to be able 'to sort it out' whereas more of the girls wanted 'to be listened to and helped'. These findings are very similar to those of the recent ChildLine Study on this topic (MacLeod 1996).

Like Howie Feel, our experience suggests that worries about achieving at school, passing exams and concerns about their future are more common amongst boys than girls.

In Howie Feel girls mention the importance of their appearance, their clothes and their body shape much more than boys do. Again this is in line with our experience at ChildLine: our counsellors hear from girls for whom such concerns have become quite extreme and who talk of dieting and sometimes quite severe eating problems.

At ChildLine there are regular and often very distressed calls from girls about their 'fall outs' with their friends, particularly their best friend. This is echoed in Howie Feel.

Drugs and alcohol

Are drug and alcohol problems as prevalent as they are reported to be? In common with Howie Feel, at ChildLine Scotland we don't hear from many young people with problems about their own drug or alcohol use. We hear from slightly more young people about negative effects of alcohol rather than drugs, usually when they have done something embarrassing while under the influence or are worried about having had unprotected sex. We do hear, however, from large numbers of young people about parental alcohol abuse affecting their lives. Such drinking is often associated with violence towards the young person.

Whilst some young people do look for factual information on drugs, the major concern about young people's drug taking seems to be an adult preoccupation. An issue for all of us is how to communicate these concerns in a meaningful way to young people when they are not apparently shared by them.

Supporting young people

A very clear message comes through from Howie Feel about young people's need to be listened to and to be seen as an individual. Young people at this age have a need to explore their world, increasingly set some of their own boundaries and develop independence. This relates directly to what we hear day in and day out, almost no matter what the young person's main reason for phoning has been. They are struggling with a variety of complex relationships and emotions. They also need to feel secure and loved which can help to give them the confidence to go out into the world and experiment safely. There is also clear evidence that, with the necessary information, young people can, and do, have valuable and considered views on a wide range of issues. We could all benefit from taking these into account more often.

In Howie Feel there were interesting comments on the completion of the questionnaire, including the ones that appear to be 'wind-ups'; we too receive the inevitable wind-ups on our phone lines. There would be something very strange going on if no young person responded in this way. There are so many possible reasons for this, including not trusting the recipients to safeguard their confidentiality, testing out what will happen, not wanting to look more closely at themselves and their lives and also having fun which is, hopefully, still an important part of being young! Some also commented about the value and benefits of being heard, of having space to work out their feelings and of someone asking and taking an interest in them. This is the ethos on which ChildLine is based: 'How I feel today is very happy for telling someone your feelings and no-one knowing in school! Thanks for listening.'

However, for some of the Howie Feel respondents, confidentiality was a concern. This is why young people call 0800 1111. At this number ChildLine offers young people a chance to speak confidentially, without being 'judged'. They are listened to and taken seriously, with the possibility of retaining control of what, if anything, happens as a result of their conversation.

Reading the Howie Feel accounts has been a joy. It has given me a glimpse of young people's lives when things are going well or well enough for them.

Even though we tend to hear from those young people who are experiencing particularly high levels of distress, Howie Feel has confirmed again that what we hear at ChildLine Scotland is representative of issues affecting young people generally.

CHAPTER 16

Inner Voices, Distant Lives?

Sally Butler

A reading of the responses to the Howie Feel Questionnaire allows us to eavesdrop on the inner voices of young people. Some of the things we hear are alarming: 'I feel tired today and unhappy, bored, depressed, lonely, frustrated, sick, unconfident, bitter, terrible, trapped, moany and very stressed'; some are reassuringly ordinary: 'I've got my ice-cream run, that will get me a bit of money so I'm sure I can afford the new Bon Jovi CD'; some we have heard many times before: 'I'm confused, I'm bored'. How do we distinguish 'normal' adolescent turbulence from real vulnerability? What are the stresses and what skills do young people have for overcoming them? Perhaps, most importantly, how can we, as adults in their lives, help them?

Normal development – 'Being a teenager is hard'
Some commentators view the life of any individual as a series of stages, each of which imposes certain tasks or tensions to be resolved. These stages can be characterised by changes in roles and often these changes involve adding new roles to existing ones, for example from husband to father. Adolescence is widely found to be troublesome because it involves so many crucial transitions. Such changes include:

- developing sexuality

- transition from family of origin to peer group and wider society

- parental control to self control

Sally Butler is a Consultant Clinical Psychologist, with a particular interest in child and adolescent health and the prevention of mental health problems, at the Royal Hospital for Sick Children, Glasgow.

○ dependence to independence.

Some would argue that mental health depends to a greater or lesser extent on how well these tasks and tensions have been resolved.

These transitions would be difficult enough if there was a gradual progression from one 'stage' to another. However, this progression is not so orderly. In Howie Feel, a girl who, in one line, demands adult independence: 'I want to escape from my parents telling me what to do and constantly trying to rule my life', by the next line sounds like a bewildered child in search of magic answers: 'I wish something or someone would make everything all right'.

Young people are expected to manage these transitions at the same time as take exams, establish their own identities in a complex peer group, embark upon steady (or shaky) sexual relationships and make important decisions about their future. It is not surprising then that what makes them feel good or bad about themselves revolves around these themes.

Feeling good or bad – 'Sometimes I hate myself and sometimes I don't'

Overwhelmingly it is school that dominates: doing well or badly in lessons and feeling stressed or overburdened by school work. The results of the Howie Feel questionnaire showed that 37 per cent felt good when they were doing well in school. Running a close second are feelings surrounding a whole host of seemingly unrelated topics, such as achievements, looks, personality and clothes. On closer inspection, however, they are all linked to a quest for value and self-worth.

It is interesting to find that gender differences regarding these preoccupations are depressingly predictable. For girls, feeling bad is largely an internal process depending on how they perceive others to be feeling about them or to be judging them. How they look is a particularly sensitive area: 'I really hate myself cause I am fat and ugly. I feel like killing myself sometimes cause I hate myself so much no one loves me'. For boys, their value of themselves is more of an external process which depends on their own actions and is more likely to be expressed physically. They also seem more wary and uncomfortable with expressed emotion: 'Rubbish, failure, hopeless, stupid, angry and want to inflict pain on somebody'.

These gender differences lead to different ways of being vulnerable. Girls seem more at risk of depression due to social factors:

> Well recently I was at the doctor's with depression and I was so uptight…
> I wish I could move away and never come back because my school and
> my home and where I live'. Girls are also more likely to engage in
> self-harming activities: 'I think I want to become anorexic because I am
> depressed about my weight'. Boys seem more at risk of antisocial

behaviours or dangerous activities: 'I enjoyed smashing those windows and throwing a banger into the shop'.

Girls and boys also have different ways of coping: girls are more likely to express and confide how they feel and boys are more likely to judge themselves positively and take action more readily. What they all find irksome is the boredom, monotony and lack of control in their lives: 'Every day I wake up and get ready for school, go to school, come home from schools then go to bed, etc. I want a change, something different to do (I'm bored with my life)'.

The sense of having no control is a constant refrain through these pages for young people and clearly contributes to how good or bad young people feel about their lives. There is some evidence from what causes stress in the workplace that whilst a high powered executive is at risk of stress, there is a greatest risk to those workers who have little or no control over their lives. There is increasing recognition that human beings function best when they themselves have a say in the structures and rules that govern their lives. Lack of control produces either helplessness and depression or rebellion and delinquency. However, adults often feel compelled to provide control because they so fear the risks to which young people are exposed.

Identifying those at risk – 'I keep wondering if I'm normal or not'

Fears about being labelled as different may prevent young people from asking for help. The signs that they are in trouble are difficult to recognise, so by the time the signals become clear and unambiguous it may mean they may have gone too far in acting on their feelings. Is it possible to identify those young people who might be at risk of becoming overwhelmed?

An obstruction to doing so lies in the very nature of the lives of young people. They lead distant lives, often fragmented between school, home and friends. Secondary education itself is fragmentary because of the number of teachers and subjects. The result may be that it is difficult for adults to have an overall perspective on the stresses in a young person's life.

Stress itself is also a hard factor to judge. Young people are making significant life transitions which cannot be achieved without a certain amount of turmoil and discomfort. Some stress, therefore, is developmentally necessary. Any change produces anxiety but helps drive motivation. Stress which is well managed increases self-esteem when it is overcome. Too much stress can prevent action and led to a loss of self-esteem. Individuals vary in temperament and therefore vary in the amount of stress they can cope with. Young people have different ways of expressing stress. It can be equally hard to recognise stress in a withdrawn young person who causes no bother as it is to recognise it in one who is defiant and aggressive. Chronic or frequent stresses may be harder to manage but more difficult to recognise than one major stress.

Risk assessment depends, therefore, on knowing individuals and in watching and listening. Indicators of trouble might be the number of settings in which difficulties are displayed or the length of time over which problems are noticed.

Prevention

We need to be able to identify those at risk, but also understand what helps young people manage stress well and hopefully prevent long-term problems. In considering the question of prevention it would be helpful to know why some who are at risk still manage to do well. What are the characteristics of these individuals or their surroundings which give them protection? These concepts of risk and resilience are just as important when it comes to understanding vulnerability in mental health. It may be possible to identify what places young people at risk – such as exposure to violence or conflict, loss of a significant carer, exploitation or abuse, poverty, etc – but frequently these factors are outside of the control of individuals who influence the daily lives of young people. It may be more productive to try to identify what creates resilience. An important element in resilience to mental health problems seems to be self-esteem. If we were able to understand how self-esteem is developed and maintained it would be useful in our attempts to help young people.

Development of self esteem – 'Everybody else's life seems so perfect'

A fundamental difference between those who function well and manage to resolve the tasks of adolescence and those who have more problems seems to lie in their sense of themselves and their view of the way the world operates.

We each see and interpret the world differently. The interpretations we make are determined by many influences: family attitudes, temperament, experience, etc. An important element in self-esteem (and thus in mental health) is the ability to interpret the world both realistically and positively. It is the difference between seeing a glass as half full or half empty. The fluid in the glass remains the same but the attitude to it is very different.

It is not just a simple distinction between pessimism and optimism. How we explain cause and effect to ourselves is even more vital. If two young people achieve the same result in an exam, one may see it as failure and the other as success and both can choose different explanations for the same result. For example, if the result is viewed as a failure, the young person may choose to blame his or herself, others, fate, etc. which, in turn, will shape their views on what to do to change the outcome. Young people who habitually choose to blame themselves in a way that is unchangeable (I'm stupid) will be more likely to feel badly about themselves, compared to those who blame themselves in a way that is changeable (I didn't do enough work). The explanation that s/he selects is important for self-esteem as well as future motivation and action. This, in turn, affects the chances of a successful or unsuccessful outcome if the same or similar situation is faced again.

Low self-esteem can so quickly lead to problem solving strategies that only compound the difficulties: giving up, avoiding, delaying, denying that it matters (I don't care), making impulsive choices, playing the clown, cheating, lying, scapegoating (bullying or blaming others). All of these behaviours exasperate adults (and peers) and are likely to attract further criticism and isolation. How quickly or slowly a view of self develops that sees the world in terms of blame, fate or distrust does depend to some extent on everyday experience and feedback.

'Help us teenagers'

Building self-esteem

Resilience to stress seems, in part, to be bound up with self-esteem. Young people who are in the process of developing these explanations of their successes and failures are particularly vulnerable to what is told to them about themselves. They are dependent on good feedback from those around them to help them construct a respectful view of themselves. As adults, we can help them build a healthy view of themselves by giving them:

- A view that helps them to see that errors and mistakes are not just acceptable but are regarded as an essential part of learning: 'I went home from school depressed but confident that my Mum would be pleased (with an exam mark) even if I wasn't'.

- Opportunities for making choices and decisions: 'You have to try things out for yourself, not to be told to do this because you need to try things'.

- A sense that along with choice comes responsibility and, therefore, guidelines are needed regarding the consequences, outcomes and implications involved in different choices. In Howie Feel young people often linked feeling good or bad about themselves to making good choices: 23 per cent felt good if they were nice to people or helpful to others and 13 per cent felt bad if they were not good or did wrong; 11.5 per cent felt bad if they argued or were cheeky to parents.

- Positive feedback through compliments and recognition of effort or achievement. This can have a significant impact on young people's mood state and ability to cope with other aspects of their lives: 'I was pleased because my science teacher said that I have been doing well in my recent work'; 'In maths the teacher was shouting at me because

I couldn't understand a sum he asked me, I felt really upset, I don't want to go to maths again'.

Giving young people a voice

Young people need opportunities to be listened to. However, they do not make it easy. They are often intensely private and prefer the company of their inner world or confide in their peers. Along with the young person's need to be understood is the conviction that they never can be: 'She (mother) says she knows what it is like to be 14 but I don't think she does, she couldn't possibly'.

Along with the demand to be listened to is their frequent refusal to explain themselves: 'Folk just won't leave me alone'.

Along with their need for advice is their belief that they know everything: 'I want to be treated like an adult'.

Giving advice

Giving advice is a tricky business however much someone might appear to need it. It has been my clinical experience that, in general, people only listen to advice which confirms the course of action they wish to take themselves anyway. Also, it is extremely difficult to give advice which covers every eventuality. In giving advice you run the risk of being held responsible for any unsuccessful outcome, or having it rejected. There is an added risk in giving advice to adolescents since it so often seems to propel them into an opposite action. We give young people advice because we want them to learn and we reason that it would be better for them to learn from our experience rather than from their own. Unfortunately, learning cannot always be achieved in this way.

In order to learn the way through a strange town, it is better to explore alone and ask directions when we need them than it is to follow a native. The more active the experience and self-correcting our errors, the faster we learn. In giving advice we sometimes fail to engage with young people in a dialogue about their lives and how they feel about themselves. Our own anxiety inhibits our ability to listen; a frequent response to the cry from the girl who feels herself to be fat is to tell her not to be silly and to eat her dinner.

It is my own experience that it is more profitable to think in terms of showing interest rather than offering advice, in giving information rather than lecturing, and to put at the centre of any communication the search for any opportunity to enhance self-esteem. If we cannot control all the risks then we should try to build resilience by helping them to make good decisions, to protect themselves by their own behaviour, to recognise the good guys from the bad guys, not because we say so but because they have a sense of their own self-worth and trust their own judgement.

Figure 16.1   *Heather Miller*

Celebration

Other aspects of young people's lives that seem to form protection when experiencing stresses are such things as rituals, festivals, special occasions and rites of passage. Opportunities to mark events or transitions in their lives are important and should be encouraged – they provide distraction, something to look forward to, recognition and a sense of belonging to a group.

Planning ahead

Helping young people themselves to be aware of stress and to recognise its effects would be useful and would give them a skill that they will need throughout their lives. Likewise, we should be teaching young people about stress and developing skills in task setting, planning and reviewing their goals. Most traditional opportunities are generally done under some pressure such as homework or exams.

'We all cope though'

Several times whilst reading the Howie Feel responses I speculated on what might be the discrepancy between the inner and outer lives of these young people. There is a sense sometimes that they find it difficult to expose themselves and that keeping up appearances is an important part of coping. The jokey exteriors and bravado may hide so much insecurity and may be a form of reassurance and distraction – to have a laugh with mates is, after all, what most of us do.

The young people's sense of perspective was also reassuring. Most seem able to achieve some balance between the good and bad. They may hate school but it is made bearable by their friends, they may have troubles at home but a good mark can lift them, and a good result in football goes a long way.

CHAPTER 17

School Days
The Best Days of Your Life?

George Potter

There is too much pressure put on 3rd years, you hear nothing but your standard grade exams. I am scared. I hate it when adults say 'school days are the best days of your life.' Well obviously they never got piled with homework. [f]

Young people are forever questioning the belief of adults that 'school days are the best days of your life'. Adults tend to remember the good days at school. What's too painful to remember, we simply choose to forget. Young people in school are, however, living the reality, not the memory, and they don't have the luxury of time and fading recollections.

In this chapter I will consider the Howie Feel Survey in relation to its implications for teachers and schools in general. What are young people saying about school and how can those of us employed in education respond to the voices of these teenagers?

Do we dare to listen? Can we afford not to?

Many times I've heard young people say teachers just don't listen. In Howie Feel, a number of young people make similar complaints:

I feel that teachers should have more of a sense of humour. I think that punishment exercises should be destroyed and that teachers should also listen to the pupils, just like we have to listen to them [m]

George Potter is a principal teacher of guidance, and a person-centred therapist, at Cathkin High School, Glasgow.

Howie Feel is a first step to providing many young people with an opportunity to have their say. It also however provides *us* with an opportunity to *listen*. Teachers may well ask: 'Is this information reliable?' After all, anonymous questionnaires are wonderful for 'wind-ups'. Isn't Howie Feel the perfect chance for pupils to have a 'go' at teachers without fear of reprisal?

So, do we just ignore what the young people say because it is too hard for us to hear or because we disagree with their points of view? If we brush aside the adolescent voice on school, we must surely brush aside all of Howie Feel. Is all of the information so unreliable?

Certainly, the nature of what has been written in Howie Feel about school is consistent with my own experience of what young people say. If we don't listen to what is being said then we run the risk of alienating our young people even more. Absence and misbehaviour in class are running at an all time high. We ask pupils to listen to us, so that they can learn. Perhaps if we listen then *we* can also learn and go some way towards improving the school situation for our young people. Maybe it's time to look after the horse before it bolts!

Perceptions of reality – who's to blame?

> School can be annoying because sometimes the teachers just can't seem to understand us [f]

Perhaps one of the major problems in school is the differing perceptions between teachers and pupils in relation to both work rate and behaviour. The following quote from the Howie Feel data illustrates this point:

> I have been in trouble twice, I feel very angry about it because the first time all I did was yawn and the teacher said I was making unnecessary noises [m]

As well as being a teacher, I am a pool lifeguard trainer/assessor. The main job of a pool lifeguard is accident prevention and, in order to do this effectively, s/he must be aware of the risk factors that will occur on the poolside and take the appropriate action to prevent any accidents happening.

I believe that teachers have a similar responsibility for prevention and should, therefore, be aware of the risk factors that will occur within the school and classroom and take the appropriate action to prevent incidents or escalation of difficulties. Teachers should be aware of the young people's home lives or family circumstances, personal relationship problems, etc. We teachers also need to consider the degree to which the learning environment we create is motivating and appropriate. Furthermore, as teachers, we must be aware of the fact that our own disposition and personal circumstances are themselves risk factors to the learning situation. How many of us will admit to coming into school in a bad mood before stepping into the classroom?

How do we acquire information on young people's risk factors? There are the formal channels of information available: guidance personnel and 'pupils at risk' lists. However, we can always ask the young people themselves.

Is there a place for happiness in learning? Does it matter?

The Howie Feel survey suggests that for many of our young people, school isn't always a happy place to be. Too much homework, exams, not doing well, etc., all take their toll on feelings about school.

I have no doubt that being happy in school increases motivation and, therefore, aids learning. Just as a radio receiver will pick up signals more readily from clear blue skies than in a cloudy thunder storm, so too will our minds be more receptive to learning if we are feeling well balanced with minimal emotional interference.

Learning to love yourself – Do schools have a responsibility?

In Howie Feel we see the wide range of issues that affect the way young people feel about themselves. School issues play their part also and there are numerous examples of how aspects of schooling impinge on the self-esteem of our young people:

> Some subjects at school can bring me down a bit because of the way some of my teachers treat me. For example, if I was to get a bad mark in a test or get into trouble they would not give me a second chance, they would treat me as being stupid or a bad pupil who is always getting into trouble [m]

> I feel good about myself about what I have achieved in school because I have good marks for my tests and I am in good rated classes [m]

Of course, pupils are people with lives outside the classroom and outside the school and are affected by feelings about their body image, their personalities, what others think about them, the actions of those important to them and such like – all of which cannot be turned off when they step inside the school gates.

Should schools have a responsibility to nurture and develop the self-esteem of young people? Do we have the time and energy to consider all these other factors when we are busy with curriculum requirements?

Before I consider these issues, I would like to cite a study which looks at the self-esteem of school pupils. A group of teachers were trained to offer higher levels of interpersonal skills in the anticipation that the pupils of these teachers would feel better about themselves than the pupils of those teachers who had not received training. After training there were differences between the two groups of pupils but, alarmingly, part of these differences were due to the fact that those pupils taught by teachers who had not received the training actually felt worse about themselves than they did at the start!

'Certainly, teaching people to like themselves less is not a process that we felt should be going on in schools.'[1]

In my work with young people I have found that self-esteem is something that seems to be in short supply for a large number of pupils. I believe that it is imperative that schools accept responsibility for developing the self-esteem of pupils and play a key role in taking care of our young people's emotional health. The rest of this chapter will focus on how I believe this can be done.

Supporting young people in schools

Developing self-esteem can be done through specialised programmes in Social Education, but that in itself is not enough. Self-esteem has to be seen as a responsibility for all teachers at all times and should be continually promoted in the classroom.

The qualities which a teacher brings to the classroom can have a profound Influence. Ideally, these qualities include:

- ° acceptance, particularly for the young person
- ° genuineness, to be fair and consistent in attitude and treatment of the young person
- ° understanding, to be aware of what it feels like for the young person in their particular circumstance.

The most influential quality, in my experience, is acceptance. If a teacher can show acceptance then maybe the young person can begin to accept his or her self. If a teacher can accept the young person as they are without being evaluative or judgmental then perhaps more effective learning can take place.

Sometimes, as teachers, we tend to forget the whole person and think that our *subject* is the most important thing in the world, forgetting that the young person may have different priorities. Making 'mistakes' in the classroom is not the end of the world but pupils are often made to feel that it is. For some, such rejection and non-acceptance can lead to the end of *their* world, however. Feelings of loneliness and inadequacy can have serious consequences and can

---

1   Rogers 1983, p.204.

be the root cause of many anti-social behaviours: bullying, truancy, misbehaviour in class, membership of gangs, etc.

Of course we must consider the curricular requirements (for many, the sole purpose of school), but not to the exclusion or suppression of the emotional self. In fact, I believe that using a person centred approach enables the curricular requirements to be met more readily. If a teacher can be his or her self in the classroom, can be genuine, then the pupils will become more relaxed, more trusting, more willing to be themselves and, therefore, more amenable to learning. If a teacher can be more understanding of the pupil, can be aware of what it feels like to be that person, then perhaps the pupil will be more willing to take risks, be more creative and be more understanding of the learning process.

Research has shown that some teachers cannot maintain eye contact with another person for more than a moment. Some pupils never receive favourable eye contact from a teacher, receiving only negative eye contact when they are being disruptive. Because of this, one school attempted to increase eye-to-eye contact over an academic year – which resulted in attendance increasing significantly. (Rogers 1983, p.210)

Eye-to-eye contact is only one way of letting young people know they are valued. Without a doubt, building self-esteem is essential for the well-being of young people: they must be given responsibility, be empowered, be encouraged to make their own decisions; they need to feel appreciated, loved, listened to, to feel they have worth; they need to feel skilful, be able to do things – if only a few things – well.

Pupil support systems

Is the Guidance system adequate for the pupils needs? Are pupil support systems necessary? Is there a need for a counselling system?

> I wish I could just get away. I just feel so depressed. I just can't cope with the work at school. Suicide would be the easiest thing. I hate my life! [f]

Howie Feel accounts reflect much the same feelings held by many of the young people that I have worked with. They are saying: 'I have these feelings, I don't understand them, I don't know what to do with them, but I have them. Who can I tell? Who can I trust?' In the Howie Feel questionnaire very few mentioned teachers.

The support mechanism in Scottish schools is mainly though the Guidance system. However, the Report of the Scottish Central Committee on Guidance (1986) states that: 'the responsibility for guidance is by no means restricted to the guidance staff; all teachers have a part to play' (p.2)

The committee discussed the principle of the school as a *caring community* and came to the understanding that this was central to the role of guidance in the secondary school:

> Caring, we believe, is more than intuitive feelings of concern or sympathetic attitudes. It is rooted in the belief that all people have value in their own right, and that their feelings, opinions and actions are important, whether or not they correspond to those of others. In practice this means that caring individuals are prepared to communicate honestly and openly with each other and enter into genuine sharing relationships. Further, it means placing confidence and trust in the capacity of others to take responsibility for themselves, their behaviour, their feelings, their attitudes and their learning. It is this recognition of the worth of the individual that is at the root of the concept of a caring community. (Scottish Central Committee on Guidance 1986, p.3)

The philosophy of the report acknowledges the needs of the young people, yet these needs are not being met. It would appear that the philosophy and the practice are quite different.

It is taking, and will take, time for schools to adjust and adapt to the principles expressed in the report. Many schools now have guidance policies which reflect its ethos and additional systems need to be set up to cope with the more extreme difficulties of some young people. One very effective way of dealing with these difficulties is by means of pupil 'support groups'.

Support groups

Support groups should be part of a whole-school approach to guidance and are there to assist young people who are having difficulty in coping. The group is there primarily to give the young people time out, a place where they are free to be themselves, a place where they will not be judged or evaluated and, therefore, are free to make their own decisions and take responsibility for those decisions.

In my experience, as a facilitator of school-based support groups, I have found that the young people who attend have several characteristics in common: they have low self-esteem, very little self-confidence and are highly sensitive to feeling. They are also very caring and highly empathic. However, they are very suspicious and distrustful of adults. I have also found that they have a very strong desire to change their present way of being.

Most school-based support groups have a 'focus'. This could be bullying, truanting, etc. I have found that a much more effective way of working with groups is to use a person-centred approach with no fixed agenda or focus. This way the 'leader' becomes a facilitator and, in fact, does not 'lead'. This implies that the power source lies not with the facilitator but with the group. This has serious implications for the person who is the facilitator as the effectiveness of the work depends largely on the relationship established and on the qualities of the facilitator. These qualities are as mentioned earlier in the chapter: acceptance, genuineness and understanding.

I have had a great deal of success using this person-centred approach in support groups, and this is commended by HM Inspectors of Schools in their report following an extended inspection of the school where I work. I now use this approach in the classroom – with equal success.

Support groups used for controlling behavioural problems in class should, in my opinion, be seen as a short-term solution. There may be pupils who have deep-rooted personal problems that will be surfacing in serious antisocial behaviour and these difficulties have to be dealt with differently, perhaps by including a counselling unit within the school support system.

Counselling unit

Counselling Units in schools can have many advantages, such as offering a high degree of confidentiality, long interview times, etc. I use the word 'counselling' in a therapeutic sense rather than in a careers or guidance interview context. I have seen a total of 52 pupils over a total of 172 hours. With six exceptions, all of those attending had problems with misbehaviour in school. For 50 of these pupils the underlying cause of their difficulty was loss, either through death, separation or divorce, of a significant adult in their life. Many of the young people are now self-referred, testimony to the trust that can be generated using a person-centred approach.

With misbehaviour in school seemingly on the increase, it may seem strange that I have suggested that support groups, used for controlling this problem, should be seen as a short-term solution. It is my opinion, based on my work with pupils both in support groups and on a one-to-one basis, that the educational system is not meeting the needs of these young people and that we need to examine how we go about the business of trying to teach them. Maybe it is the teaching we need to look at – maybe we put too much focus on teaching and not enough on *learning*. Perhaps teacher training should be geared to creating facilitators of learning, rather than teachers and lecturers. Perhaps we should be looking towards giving young people the freedom to learn.

Figure 17.1   *Adam Ross*

Freedom to learn

Does the education system adequately meet the needs of the young people or is it geared only to meet the needs and demands of society? Does this create the ideal learning environment for all young people?

There can be no doubt that our present government looks on our schools as a means of meeting the demands of society and is the ideal mechanism to cream off the 'elite'. I can think of no other reason for national testing and setting of pupils. It most certainly is not pupil centred and creates unnecessary stress and poor self-esteem for very many of our young people:

> I feel like everyone expects me to do really well in tests and stuff and if I don't, I feel ashamed of myself. I feel like I have to do better than my friends in tests because then I will still be liked. I think most of my friends feel like that too! [f]

I wonder if 'doing well at school' is so important in Howie Feel because it's the only behaviour we reward in schools. What then are the implications for the self-esteem of those who do not do well?

I have quoted previously from *Freedom To Learn for the 80s* and do so again without apology, as much can be learned from the research obtained by Carl Rogers:

> To sum it all up, the research evidence clearly indicates that when students' feelings are responded to, when they are regarded as worthwhile human beings capable of self-direction, and when their teacher relates to them in a person-to-person manner good things happen. To the consortium researchers, it seems that children who are in person-centred classrooms learn some important things about themselves, which makes it possible for them to grow more healthily and achieve more effectively. In short, students learn that they can learn, and in doing so they are free to become productive and involved – more fully functioning in every way. (1983, p.209)

My own findings, from working in a person-centred way, although not the subject of controlled research, are very similar.

Conclusion

Rather than writing my own conclusion to this chapter, I would prefer to finish with a poem from a first-year girl. Along with those voices in Howie Feel, it reminds us that pupils are real people with real feelings:

The World Inside You

Your mind can be clear
Or full of thoughts
Like the sky, with clouds or without
Your heart like a captured whale
dying to be free
Your feelings are like plants
growing and unable to control.
Life is like a tree
We grow, bloom, and then one day we die

Karen Batey

CHAPTER 18

Happy Families?

Mary Ross

Teenagers are often viewed as 'aliens' by adults in general and parents in particular – they are the mysterious element bringing a new challenge into family life. To a certain extent, whether the emergence of teenagers into the family arena contributes to the overall happiness or unhappiness of the family depends on the adults' ability to welcome rather than reject such a challenge. As family life is a recurring issue in Howie Feel, this chapter will concentrate on the nature of the relationship between teenagers and their parents and offer some suggestions as to how the relationship can be enhanced for all parties.

Judging parents: a good thing?

As children grow towards adulthood they develop their critical thinking powers. By this means they are able to stand back from the other members of the family and take a long hard look at the behaviour they see around them. It can be very disarming for parents to hear their teenage offspring pass comment on how they as parents are performing in many aspects of family and personal life. It takes a very secure adult not to over-react when they come under the watchful gaze of an adolescent who is 'playfully' exercising their new critical faculty. If the parent is not feeling personally secure and confident, each criticism levelled at them undermines their own authority; if they take the teenager's comments too seriously, they feel under personal attack and are likely to retaliate. Many of the conflicts which occur between teenagers and their parents can find their origin here. If it was possible for parents to recognise that being critical is an important part of growing up, they are more likely to

---

Sister Mary Ross is an educational psychologist and Director of the Notre Dame Child Guidance Clinic and Adolescent Unit, Glasgow.

be able to welcome the development of this ability and find ways of not taking on board *personally* any criticism that comes their way. The 'Dear Diary' accounts in the Howie Feel survey give many examples of how teenagers may view their parents' behaviour. Some of these relate to the way parents communicate with their teenagers, others have more to do with the effects of their parents' lifestyles on them. For example:

> My mum has been frustrating me, she thinks she knows how to talk to me because she is a Counsellor. She is so patronising and she only wants to know what I am doing that I shouldn't.

> Today has been really bad and boring. I suppose it's just really me that can change though, but I feel as if I can't because of my problems. I know it is nobody else's fault but I feel as if it is Mum, it's her drinking and everything else that she does.

> My mum sometimes criticises me and it makes me feel as if she can't accept me for who I am.

If the adults being described here cannot cope when their teenage sons and daughters comment on their behaviour, arguments or feuds tend to be the result. It is difficult for parents to realise that when their teenager is struggling towards adulthood it is vital for them to examine the behaviour of those adults closest to them in order to make up their own minds about how they will live their own adult lives in the future.

In my experience, statements and criticisms from teenagers are best heard as questions and can thus be dealt with by parents recognising that their son or daughter is now at a stage where they want to know how to make adult decisions. Although it is not necessary for parents to discuss *all* their private and personal matters with their sons or daughters, it is helpful if they can begin to explore with them some of the reasons behind their own behaviour. Sometimes it is a good idea to allow the teenager to comment on what they experience as the consequences of their parents' behaviour. For example, some of the diary comments indicated that they actually knew that the reason their parents were 'nagging' them was because they were concerned. However, these comments were often accompanied by feelings that this concern was suffocating. For example:

> I also feel loved by my parents but feel they do not give me privacy all of the time. They like to always know what I'm doing every minute of the day.

The normal stresses of life today can lead to parents and teenagers finding it difficult to talk to one another as equals. Yet making space for one-to-one chats can be very important to a growing teenager. This helps them understand how their parents 'tick'. It does, however, require considerable skill on the parents' part to choose appropriate timing for such a chat and parents should try not to feel too rejected if teenagers don't immediately jump at the chance!

Becoming independent

Teenagers are aware that once they become adults they have to stand on their own two feet and make their own decisions. It is only natural that parents are wary of some of their teenagers' attempts to do this too soon. Often the reason that parents appear to be over-protective or hypercritical of their teenagers is that they are genuinely frightened by some of the behaviours they produce. The majority of resulting conflicts are caused by the teenagers' belief that they have a right to do their own thing and the parents' corresponding fear that this will lead to some negative experiences for their youngster. This is reflected in some of the Howie Feel comments:

> I don't want restrictions from my parents, I want to make my own decisions. I feel I am old enough to do what I want.

> I wish I was allowed out late but I am constantly getting told 'it's not safe' for example. I want to be treated more like an adult.

If the parents of teenagers tried to argue them out of this way of thinking it would be perfectly understandable because the adults themselves know how difficult it is to make right decisions all of the time. They would naturally be afraid that these teenagers may not seek appropriate advice. It is certainly not easy to appreciate this 'in-between' stage that a teenager is in – they do not require the same amount of protection as a child and yet they are not absolutely sure what is best for them, but have to sound as if they do! In such a situation I have found that the best way forward is to try to keep open the lines of communication between parent and teenager. This way the teenager knows that the parent is there, not so much to always tell them what they can and cannot do but to help them explore some of the possible consequences of their behaviour before they actually occur.

The meaning of life…

Young people develop their ability to think in the abstract as they grow through their mid-teen years. This allows them to take quite a philosophical approach to life, reflecting on what is important to them and others around them. It can be a joy to a parent to see this capacity emerge and develop. However, as with all the gifts that we have, exercising them can have both positive and negative effects. One of the most frightening aspects of this new-found ability in teenagers is the way in which they can reflect on the purpose of their own lives.

When we combine this with their awareness of intense feelings, it can be very upsetting and worrying for parents when teenagers describe themselves, if only to their diaries, as follows:

> I just want to kill myself sometimes. I wish something or someone would make everything alright.

> I was fighting with my Mum and Dad and I feel really down about things. I wish I could be in a Home and I feel like giving up or killing myself.

Teenagers will often say that they want to leave home, escape, kill themselves or just 'get out' of the situation. It is vital to take such expressions of hopelessness seriously, but not to panic about them. These are not idle comments, but neither are they necessarily expressions of suicidal intentions.

In my experience, parents are best not to indicate that they know how their teenage son or daughter is feeling because they have 'been there' themselves:

> She says she knows what it is like to be 14 but I don't think she does, she couldn't possibly.

Rather, I would advise that parents make some space for the teenager to talk about how he or she actually feels. It is important not to pressurise young people into talking about very difficult personal intense feelings but rather to show that there is an open invitation for these feelings to be discussed. We should remember that adults often contain their feelings, whereas teenagers tend to act them out more readily; they have a tendency to express them in quite an exaggerated way, for example the teenagers who describe themselves as follows:

> I just want to blow up.

> I feel angry, confused, depressed, and ready to explode.

It is important for adults not to be frightened off by such intense emotion but rather to show that they are interested in hearing what has led up to these feelings.

A testing time

Adolescence is a time of varied experimentation, as new identities and possible selves are tried on for size. Current educational practice has fed into this by encouraging young people to take part in work experience during their compulsory school years so that they can have a 'taste' of future careers. Usually parents are happy with *this* type of experimentation and may probably wish this was the end of it! However, their teenage sons and daughters may also experiment with drug taking, under-age sexual behaviour and other high-risk physical activities. Some may also enjoy the 'buzz' of exploring the delinquent side of life. Parents of such teenagers are unlikely to admire this corresponding prowess which their sons and daughters are exhibiting; they are more likely to feel that their offspring are outwith their control. In this situation parents should be encouraged to seek help so that they can try to exercise appropriate authority. This is best achieved not by making idle threats that cannot be carried out but rather through helping the young person weigh up the consequences of their behaving in this way. Teenagers, in turn, can be helped to take a look at themselves critically and decide what place such behaviours are going to have in their life.

Teenagers holding centre stage

The teenage stage of life tends to be a rather self-centred one. This is not to be confused with selfishness but, rather, is a necessary aspect of this period, allowing the teenager to grow in self-knowledge. Their new-found philosophical approach to life aids this self-reflection. Some may have an unnerving tendency to expect that as they concentrate on their developmental changes, the rest of society will stay static. They may *rarely* apply their reflective powers to consider what life is like for those around them and so feel put out when parents are busy with their own preoccupations. For example:

> I feel sad because my mum takes more interest in her boyfriend than me.

Often parents and teenagers vie with one another for attention. In some families it is a parent who suddenly needs to get away from it all, to find space and time to think out personal decisions or explore their feelings. Parents have their own concerns – such as how their marriage is faring, new friendships, employment issues or financial worries. They may truly not have the time to give to a teenager who is worrying about, say, 'a fall out with a best friend'. Sometimes it takes a third party to help parents and teenagers to see what life is like from one another's point of view. Occasionally this will require professional help where a 'stranger' can enter the family circle and facilitate a shared growth in understanding. Parents should be encouraged to seek such help when they think this is necessary.

The youth of today

Teenagers have to be seen against the background of their own time. It is tempting for adults to compare today's teenagers with what they themselves were like. However, the speed of change over the last two decades means that adults have to be aware of the different demands made on today's teenagers. For example, we have a generation of 'Designer Teens' with young people who feel they can only be seen in the latest gear. Many's the parent who has gone into debt to try to keep their teenage son or daughter in the style of their friends. Although these pressures can present throughout the year, it is often at

Christmas time that the image of 'happy families' is shattered as the tensions around the financial build-up to this time of celebration burst out. Some parents have told me of the jealousy they feel when they realise that their teenage sons or daughters have more money to spend on themselves than the parents do.

It is hard for parents who, as teenagers, had to be in by 10 or 11pm to know how to cope with the requests from their sons or daughters to *go out* at that time to discos, raves, etc. Often the best way to deal with this confusing world of late nights out, designer labels, expensive computers and the latest software is for parents to talk over their concerns with other parents so that they can begin to get some sense of today's world. This might reduce the possibility of parents using their own adolescent years as the marker for comparison. It is meaningless to a teenager to have their parents constantly justify a refusal with 'I never did (had) that in my day'. Parents merely open themselves up to ridicule if they use this tack.

Finally, teenagers generally see adults as very serious, having little fun and saddled with responsibilities. Growing up toward adulthood should be a joyful experience. The most effective method of learning is by imitation. After all, this is how the teenagers learnt when they were children. The best way parents and other adults can encourage young people to embrace adulthood is by modelling it as a worthwhile state to be in. If adults go around with long faces and full of 'do's and don'ts', 'musts and must nots' and with faces full of care, we should not be surprised if teenagers are reluctant or fearful to grow towards an adult approach to life. Adult life can have it's problems but if parents are able to show that these can be worked through, their teenagers will be given hope that whatever the future holds for them, there are always ways to cope with the difficulties. In this way their lives can be lived to the full.

CHAPTER 19

He Said, She Said

Susan McGinnis

When I was invited to contribute to this book I prepared myself for the task with reading and research on gender differences and adolescent development. The end result of my Howie Feel experience, however, meant setting aside the expectation of being an expert and discovering again how much I learn by now knowing, not letting preconceived ideas interfere with my understanding of what each person is saying.

Although I have worked with young people for some time, the Howie Feel survey provided me with a unique opportunity to immerse myself in their world. It was a chance for them to say, anonymously and uncensored, not only how they felt on that day but also what they do with those feelings. It was a chance for me to be in that world anonymously too, rather than as the adult I am in my one-to-one or group contacts where I am accepted but still, ultimately in their eyes, a grown up. I sat down eagerly with a huge stack of all the 'Dear Diary' pages and, as I read them, I laughed, cried, moaned in sympathy and suffered in despair. It felt chaotic and powerful yet familiar, as if I were getting a sample of the human condition rather than just the adolescent one, but through the raw honesty of those who hadn't yet learned to hold back or adjust their feelings about the confusion, pain and joy that we all experience.

The material was already separated by gender when it was given to me so I'll never know what I might be writing now had I shuffled them all together, but when I finished reading it I did feel that I had been in two very different worlds. The girls' world seemed to be busy with people and a sense of community which has its up and down sides. Their feelings had very much to

Susan McGinnis is a counsellor, with a particular interest in young people, at the University of Strathclyde, Glasgow.

do with how the others felt about them, so that when the feedback was good everything was fine and when it was bad it was awful. The boys' world, in contrast, felt more solitary, despite plenty of mates around, so that when it was good everything was fine (and Rangers/Celtic had won) but when it was bad it was lonely and a bit anxious. One of the stark and terrible statistics about teenage boys is that they have the fastest growing suicide rate of any age group. Recent research on stress indicates that people experience more stress the less support they feel around them. I wondered after reading the boys' responses whether a connection could be made between these two points and, if so, despite the fact that the Howie Feel data indicates that many boys want to be alone when they feel bad, how might we, as potential supporters, go about respecting that need but creating a context where 'alone' doesn't necessarily mean isolated.

This brings me to a difficulty I encountered while trying to respond to the Howie Feel data and with which I feel I need to preface the rest of my remarks, which are likely to be peppered with words like 'I wonder' and 'maybe'. As a counsellor I have learned that it is crucial not to make an assumption that I understand what anyone means by even the simplest words like 'good' or 'bad'. My sense, from what I read in the 'Dear Diary' material and, even more so, in the middle section of the questionnaire ('Three things which make me happy/unhappy, etc.'), was that 'good' was close to being the same for both sexes and was more or less what we all mean when we say we feel good but that 'bad' might be something else entirely.

The girls seem to be somehow more comfortable with feeling bad and say things like 'I talk to my friends/mum/aunt/gran' and 'I rent a video and eat chocolate' to feel better while the boys say things like 'I want to kill myself' and 'I want to kill someone/hurt someone/be violent' with an intensity that seems to reflect the intensity they feel when they feel bad (there were of course a full range of responses to these questions from both boys and girls and there were as many boys who wanted to be comforted as there were girls who wanted just to bash someone, but these were the ones that stood out for me). Does this have to do with that stress/support ratio? Do girls and boys experience 'bad' with equal intensity but are girls more accustomed to feeling up and down?

Or does it have to be really bad for boys to think it's worth mentioning? ChildLine's study, *We Know It's Tough to Talk* (MacLeod 1996), appears to support this idea in that when boys ring for help it tends to be with problems so serious they often require an intervention by police or social services. It may be that the stereotypical hypothesis drawn from this – boys think talking about feelings isn't macho or boys can't talk about how they feel – is true, or at least true for some. The stereotypical conclusion – boys should talk about their feelings – also might make life easier for the women in their lives. However, this isn't necessarily the right solution for boys or for those of us working with them. It is, in effect, asking them to communicate more like girls. The challenge is not to condemn boys, or beg them in desperation to tell us what is wrong, but to find ways to work with what they are telling us in the Howie Feel survey.

There is much in the Howie Feel data that *does* fit the recognised ways in which boys and girls are perceived to differ emotionally. The girls are more gregarious and rate friends, family and boyfriends as sources of the best and worst that happens to them. They are more concerned with their physical selves – their looks, their sexual development, their thinness, fatness and ugliness – and their self-esteem fluctuates consistently with how they feel about their bodies. The boys are people of action – many of them responded to the 'Dear Diary' section's invitation to 'say exactly how you feel' with a recital of what they did that day, as if to say that doing is feeling. This may simply be a way of saying that no news is good news but it may also be saying that their feelings of confidence and well-being are connected to what they do. School, sport, money, having a girlfriend, holidays and playing computer games are most important to them.

When I reflect on the things that surprised me as I read what boys and girls were saying, it is with the awareness of my own gender – the risk that I might be making assumptions about understanding the girls simply because I am/was one and unduly fascinated with the boys because I am not one. I was surprised that boys are more afraid of violence than girls are. I was surprised by the fact that the boys were so concerned about doing well in school, with a view to their future. What was poignant for me was that this worry about succeeding academically was sometimes expressed with appalling spelling and grammar. I was also surprised by the boys repeatedly saying that one of the things that makes them feel bad about themselves is getting into trouble. I have a suspicion that some of the boys who were making these responses might be the 'bad boys' – the ones who act disruptive, cheeky and tough but often feel emotionally vulnerable. I was entertained by the humour and outrageous comments, again mostly from the boys – especially the wonderfully imaginative one who gave explicit details of what he'd like to do with whoever was reading his reply if it happened to be a female. I doubt that this says that the girls are humourless; maybe it suggests that they take their feelings seriously and/or that boys use humour in expressing theirs. Most importantly for me, Howie Feel puts to rest the myth that boys can't express their feelings as well as girls can. Is it possible to distinguish the sex of these writers?

> Today I feel fed up, lonely and tired a bit angry, sick and frightened, bored, frustrated because I have been through a lot of nervous moments this past week.

> Today I feel very uncomfortable and unhappy I feel on a different level from everyone else.

Today has been really bad and boring. I suppose its just really me that can change through, but I feel as if I can't because of my problems. I know it is nobody else's fault but I feel as if it is my mum, it's her drinking and everything else that she does. I feel angry, confused, depressed and ready to explode. It is probably just part of growing up but it doesn't feel that way. I feel as if everybody is on my back, moaning all the time, just at me.

These three accounts were all written by boys.

The boys in the Howie Feel survey were a captive sample – does this tell us that they can express their feelings perfectly well but ordinarily wouldn't do so unless it's required? I got the feeling that a lot of them liked having the chance to write down how they felt and a few said so – 'This paper was good for me as I don't often get the chance to say how I feel'. Maybe Howie Feel asked the right questions or found the right way to ask them.

Something that struck me about the girls' replies was the fact that at the very extreme end of things, when really terrible things had happened (death, family problems), they felt they couldn't tell anyone. I wondered then about the silence that accompanies eating disorders and sexual abuse, and the absence of these from the Howie Feel replies. If the statistics about the prevalence of these things in this age group are anywhere near true then I suspect there is a lot they haven't said.

Some of the myths about girls are challenged by their Howie Feel responses as well. The girls' teen magazine *Sugar* was recently at the centre of controversy because of its sexual content, and in the recent crop of articles about girl gangs the tone has been the one of prurient disapproval reserved for the breaking of taboos. Girls in the Howie Feel survey feel violent and they can feel sexy. There are one or two cases where a boy says that his girlfriend wants sex but he doesn't feel ready. How ready are we to accept the violence and sexuality girls feel? And how best can we make a safe environment for them to explore these feelings without danger to themselves and others?

Howie Feel tells us many things about this group of people at such a vulnerable point in their lives and it is an extremely valuable resource. For all of their differences, the boys and girls in the survey experience emotional ups and downs; they worry about relationships, those relationships come and go, they dislike school and care about it at the same time. In their transition to adulthood, adolescents shuttle back and forth between wanting to be childlike and wanting to be treated as independent adults, a process that is bewildering for them and can leave even the closest families feeling angry and confused. Trying out adult things is both thrilling and frightening and, more often that not, what you're doing is just exactly the sort of thing you don't want to tell your parents about – even though it may also provoke the most powerful need for parental comfort and reassurance. My concern as a counsellor is with those who don't have anywhere to turn or feel that what is happening to them is too awful to share and are at risk.

As I contemplate all of these pages of statistics in the Howie Feel survey, and all of the questions I have raised in this chapter, I can feel the urge to turn it into some kind of action plan – in short, to become 'Someone Who Knows', someone with the answers. Taking the position of not knowing can be hard, especially for a parent who may feel shocked or guilty, a teacher who is overworked or a social worker faced with an ethical quandary. There is certainly a necessary place for answers, rules and guidelines – teenagers who have the security of something to rebel against generally come out better than those who don't. There is also security to be offered, however, in the position of not knowing, and that is in offering a safe context that is as free from judgement as possible. Young people are often very creative and sometimes hurtful in the way they test this acceptance, which is so at odds with the way they feel about themselves. From this point of acceptance, however, comes the possibility of being allowed to be a firm companion, if nothing else, in the fear, shame, sadness, loss, confusion, hurt and all of the rest of the emotions they feel.

CHAPTER 20

What the Doctor Ordered
The Role of the GP

Phil Wilson

Like every other 'authority figure', we GPs often have awkward relationships with adolescents. In some cases, this awkwardness may stop us offering effective care for young people in need. As well as general difficulties relating to the potential generation gap between us and young people, there are specific reasons why GPs and adolescents may find it difficult to get on well.

Almost everyone has an idea of what a consultation with a GP should be like, but everyone's ideas are different. For some 13 to 15-year-olds the idea of a visit to the GP might involve memories of being taken (more or less willingly) to the doctor by a parent. The wait in the surgery was more or less interminable and probably involved irritated parental warnings to keep quiet or to stop running around. The ten-year-old copies of *The People's Friend* hardly provided much diversion. When the child patient was eventually seen by the doctor, the parent probably described the symptoms to the doctor and the doctor in turn conducted a brief physical examination before writing a prescription for some horrible-tasting medicine, or giving an injection.

This might be termed the 'non-collaborative' model of the GP-child consultation. Clearly it is a caricature, but most GPs can probably remember consultations which have gone this way. It is particularly easy to conduct a dialogue solely with a parent when time is pressing, a common enough situation in general practice. These days, most of us would try to have at least some discussion with the young person about the presenting problem, the diagnosis and the treatment, if any. Nevertheless, much of the business of children's medicine is inevitably conducted between parent and doctor.

Dr Phil Wilson is a General Practitioner and Research Fellow with the Department of General Practice, University of Glasgow.

Consultations with adults are different in many ways. We expect to let the patient tell his or her story before we clarify some matters of fact and arrive at a shared account of the problem. We would attempt to agree a diagnostic strategy, and eventually a diagnosis would emerge. We would explain the diagnosis to the patient and then move on to some sort of negotiation about treatment, which might involve discussion about the risks and benefits of different types of therapy. There are, therefore, major differences in the way we work with children and with adults. A brief consideration of medical ethics might shed some light on just what these differences are. The four basic ethical principles of medicine might be simply expressed as:

- beneficence, or the necessity to try to do good to the patient

- non-maleficence, or the need to minimise the potential for harm

- confidentiality

- respect for autonomy.

The first two principles do not differ when applied to children, adolescents or adults. The ways we deal with confidentiality and autonomy are, however, different.

Adolescent patients are likely to find it difficult to believe that doctors will deal with information in a confidential manner. Parents were, after all, privy to all information about their children's health. This difficulty may have significant effects on health care: adolescents, when looking for advice on contraception, will often travel considerable distances to a family planning clinic, whereas most adults would attend their GP. The obvious conclusion is that young people do not trust their GP with information about their sexuality. Perhaps more often, they just do not think of us as a source of help in times of emotional or social difficulty. The Howie data suggest that professionals such as doctors are unlikely to be a support in times of crisis. Only 1 per cent said they would like it if there was a professional (other than a teacher) to speak to when they feel bad. Similarly, only a few of the young people cited a professional among people they could talk to generally.

Why could this be? A recent study among 12 to 16-year-olds revealed that reluctance to discuss things with the doctor was partly due to embarrassment and fears that the doctor would tell their parents about the nature of the consultation. Whilst it may be no surprise that sexual matters were the biggest taboo area for young people in talking to GPs, what is perhaps more significant is the fact that 'talking about feelings' came second (Greater Glasgow Health Board 1994).

One major worry for the GP is when a parent turns up with concerns about a child, but without the young person being present. A typical scenario is where the parent suspects illicit drug use. Often we are asked not to tell the young person about the consultation. This is, of course, almost impossible and the best we can do is to contact the young patient and say that the parent has expressed concern. In order to get anywhere in this situation we have to assure the adolescent that anything they say will be dealt with confidentially.

The issue of autonomy is also important in understanding the relationship between the GP and adolescent patient. Some useful insights can be found in a 1995 study of attitudes to the school-based measles/rubella immunisation campaign. Pupils aged 11 to 15 years were given a questionnaire in a research project conducted by two school pupils and a paediatrician (Rylance, Bowen and Rylance 1995). The vast majority of youngsters believed that they had enough maturity to make an informed decision about immunisation. Only one-third of the respondents believed that attending the immunisation session and holding out an arm, or being co-operative, implied consent to the vaccination. However, as only one in 20 children were asked their views and only one in 14 were asked if they gave consent at the time of receiving their injections, it seems that little value was placed on informed consent by young people, at least in the recent measles/rubella immunisation campaign.

When and why do GPs see adolescents?

Most of the problems brought to us by adolescents, or more usually by their parents, are apparently physical. The commonest reasons for consultations with 13 to 15-year-olds are: viral infections (such as gastroenteritis and influenza); skin problems (eczema, acne, warts); asthma; hayfever; migraine; accidents; and appendicitis. Although these problems might seem very different from psychiatric disorders, it should be noted that most of these 'physical' conditions can be exacerbated by stress. Furthermore, the decision to come to a doctor about a viral infection or a headache is not a simple black-and-white matter: why do most people put up with these minor physical discomforts and not consult the doctor? Much research about minor illness in adults and younger children (there is little evidence on consulting in adolescence) suggests that social and emotional factors play almost as much a part in the decision to consult as the severity of the condition itself.

Less than 5 per cent of consultations are overtly psychiatric or related to emotional disturbance: the more common types of problem here would be self-harm, anorexia nervosa or parental worries about illicit drug use. For a typical GP, this sort of consultation would happen only a handful of times each year. New presentations of major psychiatric illness, such as obsessional/compulsive disorder, or psychotic illnesses, such as schizophrenia or manic depressive illness, would only be seen by a typical GP once every ten years, or less commonly.

Almost as uncommon as the presentation of psychotic illness is the direct presentation of the more 'minor' psychiatric conditions – anxiety neurosis and depression. Yet we know from large-scale population studies that anxiety and depression are more or less as prevalent in the teenage years as at other times. In other words, we might expect about one in ten youngsters in the 13 to 15 age group to be suffering from clinical anxiety or depression; perhaps five or so individuals on a GP's list at any one time. The Howie data back this up. Statements indicating depression, for example, were fairly common in the sample.

So, why the mismatch between the number of young people who are suffering significant psychological distress at any one time and the number of times the patients come to the doctor with anxiety or depression? Apart from the fact that many distressed young people will simply not attend the GP during the episode of disturbance, the complex area of the relationship between mind and body sometimes makes diagnosis difficult.

The mind and the body: physical presentations of emotional problems

Many young people with emotional difficulties will attend with 'vague' symptoms. The nature of the distress may be social (family, school, friends), emotional, or both. For example, recent research has shown a strong association of bullying with a variety of physical symptoms. Bullying is also more likely to be aimed at children with pre-existing physical or emotional problems.

A fictitious, but realistic, case history might give some insight into the way that doctors struggle to make sense of the presentation of illness in a young person:

John McAllister is a 14-year-old patient brought by his mother to Dr Louise Jones, a new young partner in the practice. John's mother says that he has had awful diarrhoea and he just seems exhausted. He is not even interested in playing football any more and his school work is suffering. John looks like a strong enough boy, perhaps a little aggressive. Dr Jones knows that John's father has a very disabling bowel disorder called ulcerative colitis, which has had a major impact on his life: he has had a major operation and side effects from multiple courses of steroids. The doctor asks about the symptoms of the bowel disorder and if John is worried about his bowel problems. John answers that he is worried. Dr Jones examines John's abdomen and finds nothing abnormal and then does some blood tests. She asks John and his mother to come back in three weeks.

The blood tests are normal, but Dr Jones is worried that she is missing something. She refers John to a gut specialist at the local hospital. At the hospital the specialist thinks that some further investigations are needed. He arranges a telescopic examination of John's bowel, which John finds uncomfortable and embarrassing. John returns with his mother to his general practice for the results. Dr Jones is on holiday so he sees Dr Smith, the senior partner. He is reassured that all is well as far as the bowel investigation is concerned, but John's face confirms that all is not well with him as a person. Dr Smith asks about John's sleep pattern and John tells him that he keeps waking up and cannot get back to sleep. The doctor knows that this is a characteristic sleep pattern of someone who is depressed. He also knows that John's uncle died about six months ago; he remembers seeing John in the uncle's house several times when he was making visits to provide terminal care. He asks Mrs McAllister if he could have a talk with John alone and asks her to wait in the waiting room. She looks a bit uncomfortable about this but agrees.

Dr Smith says that he thought John seemed upset. He wondered what it was about. John said nothing so Dr Smith commented that it is often difficult for men to express sad feelings. John looked on the edge of tears. Dr Smith asked whether he was missing his uncle; he knew that John was close to him. He asked about the things they used to do together. John said a few words about how much he missed him and cried for about 15 minutes. At the end of this time, as the tears were abating, Dr Smith said that he thought John should come and see him once a week for a while to talk about him and his uncle. He asked if he should say anything to John's mother. John said he would rather not. John wiped away the tears and Mrs McAllister returned to the consulting room. Dr Smith said that he and John had been having a man-to-man talk and it would be helpful for the two of them to meet a few times over the next few weeks. Mrs McAllister looked uncomfortable. She asked what the problem was but Dr Smith said it was probably best kept between John and him.

Mrs McAllister returned, ostensibly with a cold, the following week. A cold is often a 'ticket of entry' to the doctor. She said that John had said he does not need to come back; he was fine. In fact he's been out playing football almost every night this week. She asked what the problem was, was it drugs or sex? Dr Smith said that all he could really say was that it was nothing Mrs McAllister need worry about.

This case illustrates a number of points. First, it is possible to formulate a problem in lots of different ways. In this case, we could make a diagnosis of irritable bowel syndrome – a common cause of diarrhoea exacerbated by stress. We could also make a psychiatric diagnosis – depression – or we could consider this a bereavement reaction. Second, knowledge of a young person's family circumstances can help us to work out what is important in a case. Third, the gender of the doctor can be relevant in some (but certainly not all) circumstances. Finally, apparent 'toughness' can be deceptive.

Detection of emotional disturbance, and prevention of mental illness

As emotional problems can be difficult to diagnose, the key factor in successful management of emotional problems in general practice may be the creation of an atmosphere where patients feel comfortable discussing emotions. This may well involve confronting significant taboos, such as talking about sex or death, in both patients and their doctors (who are also, incidentally, human beings).

Some advocate a more proactive role for GPs in situations which seem to pose risks for young people. The relationship between adverse life events and mental health problems is at least as strong in adolescents as in adults. Such adverse circumstances include: divorcing parents, bereavement, alcoholic parents and situations where adolescents are acting as carers for disabled relatives. There is little direct evidence of benefit from these sorts of interventions, and perhaps our role lies in striving to ensure that we are aware of these situations and checking out with young people how they are feeling about things.

There may be a stronger case for action in cases of deliberate overdose and other apparent suicide attempts. It is common for GPs to be notified of these by hospital casualty departments, with a note that no formal psychiatric diagnosis was made and the patient was discharged. Making some sort of contact with the young person, if only to offer the opportunity of confidential support if it should be needed later, might be useful. We need to bear in mind all sorts of reasons which could have led to the suicide attempt, such as its strong association with sexual abuse.

Conclusion: the relationship between the young person and GP and how we might make it work better

So far we have discussed some of the difficulties that GPs may have with their young patients and some of the difficulties that young people have with their GPs. Respect for confidentiality and autonomy are crucial for successful work with emotional problems in young people. There may be a case for making the nature of the doctor/patient relationship explicit to young people, who may not understand the 'rules'.

Like any group of people, GPs vary in their degree of confidence in dealing with emotional problems. As well as this general ability in helping patients to talk about emotions, the GP's level of skill may also depend on the age and gender of the patient.

It is clear from the Howie data that many young people have significant emotional problems, and in the questionnaire responses one in twelve young people said they had no-one with whom they could discuss feelings. GPs may be able to help some of these people, although it would be unrealistic to suggest that we could offer a major therapeutic input to large numbers of adolescents. Our specific strengths lie in family knowledge and in an ability to disentangle physical from emotional problems. We have access to services specialising in providing support for young people. It should be noted, however, that many young people would rather go to their local surgery, a place without stigma, than attend a mental health resource centre. Practice-based counselling might offer an acceptable compromise solution, although research evidence supporting this kind of provision would be needed to gain the substantial funding required.

Since severe psychological disturbance in adolescents is a relative rarity in general practice, the majority of cases are referred for specialist help. The nature of services available for referral varies from area to area but adolescent psychiatry services and child guidance clinics tend to be the first line of referral for most GPs. There is fairly general agreement that GPs should generally not initiate the prescribing of drugs such as antidepressants to younger adolescents, and research suggests that this happens rarely.

Howie Feel has provided us with some fascinating data on the inner worlds of adolescents, a world of which we GPs rarely get more than a glimpse. GPs can offer some help to some young people in times of difficulty but time constraints, varied levels of clinical skill and public perceptions mean we can certainly not help in every problem. Nevertheless, when there seems to be no one else to turn to, and a young person feels overwhelmed, the GP may be able to help.

CHAPTER 21

Caring for Teenagers in the 21st Century
Young Voices Matter

Graham Bryce

Whose voices are heard when services for young people are being organised and offered? There are the voices of those who work in them: teachers, youth workers, counsellors, psychologists, social workers, therapists, doctors, managers and others. There are the voices of those who have a say in the policy-making and resourcing of these services: politicians, officials and others. There are the voices of those who play a part in the day-to-day lives of young people: parents, friends, families and neighbours. Then, of course, there are the voices of the young persons themselves.

While all of these parties have a voice, some are more influential than others. Is this as it should be? Whose interests are served and whose are neglected in the distribution of influence? How do we make sure that each voice is given due respect and influence?

Howie Feel is an exercise in listening to the voices of young people. In this chapter we look at ways of allowing young voices to influence the services provided to care for them.

First of all, let's be clear: compared to employment opportunities, good housing and fairness and stability in relationships, health services, even those that are very good, have a modest effect on the quality of mental health in a community.

Second, compared to the number of people working alongside young people day in, day out, sticking with them and sticking up for them – families, friends

---

Graham Bryce is a Consultant Child and Adolescent Psychiatrist, with a particular interest in the planning and organisation of services, at the Possilpart Health Centre, Glasgow.

and professionals throughout the community – the part played by those of us who work in very specialised services is relatively small.

This isn't to say that these services are unimportant. The mental health of young people is, however, first and foremost influenced by matters that affect the whole community, and is the business of the whole community.

Mental health: everybody's business

Health is about growing and relating well, not just avoiding illness. Mental health is not about a stress-free life but about dealing with distress. But what does this mean for a community? What needs to be done to enable young people to work out this vision of mental health?

Over the next few pages, as we consider this question, we'll look at the part we all play, the matter of needing extra help, issues around getting help and the way help is organised and offered.

Anyone closely involved with a young person is likely to be making a contribution to the way that young person's life shapes up. This, for the most part, involves supporting them as they sort through what they want to do, what resources and skills they have and what opportunities are available to them. From these, and other elements, they strive to fashion a satisfactory identity – a coherent picture of who they are.

Meeting and dealing with problems is an important part of this process. When any of us has a problem it's natural to look to someone well known and trusted ('friends' and 'mums' according to Howie Feel) and to try familiar solutions ('go to my room' or 'try and cheer myself up' were amongst the most common replies). These ordinary, important steps that young people take to help them cope with their experiences are the cornerstone of supporting, promoting and ensuring mental health.

Needing help?

Sometimes, however, these steps aren't enough. There may have been some particularly distressing experiences, maybe those supportive relationships aren't available or, perhaps, those very relationships are part of the problem. Another recent study of almost a thousand young people in the West of Scotland (West and Sweeting 1996) found that at age 15 over 10 per cent of boys and more than 18 per cent of girls had high levels of emotional difficulty. Even more concerning was that three years later 33 per cent of the boys and 41 per cent of the girls were now in difficulty. So, emotional problems are not uncommon amongst adolescents. But which of them need help? What kind of help do they need? Who is best placed to provide that?

There are a few situations where it's pretty clear that extra help is needed urgently. For instance, a young person's life may be completely dominated by a problem, sometimes to the extent of putting their life in danger. That's a good indication that it's time to move quickly for professional help. These situations *do* arise for some young people but they're not the common experience. More usual are those situations where the difficulties are like exaggerations of normal experience, for example loss of confidence, major worries about appearance, feeling very unhappy, finding coping with relationships frustrating and too difficult and so on.

What then? It's clear that many young people find their way through these experiences without professional help. Many of them will turn to their friends and, with their support and encouragement, will manage to work things out. Others turn to their families and find their Mum or Gran patient and under-standing. Some will find a teacher, or a worker at the youth club has known some other young person with this kind of problem and can offer some good ideas.

Sometimes, however, supports like these are not enough and it gradually becomes clear that something else needs to be done. Making that decision is seldom easy, but actually following it through, especially if it involves going somewhere unfamiliar, is often difficult.

So, getting help involves taking a bit of a risk and often presents a dilemma: 'I need help to get confidence, but I need confidence to get help.' Those familiar with the young person, who stand alongside him or her at that point, can, therefore, find themselves playing a new part too – one where they have to say: 'I can't give you all the help you need, but I can help you find it and support you through it.'

Getting help

It's important to consider how a young person might view this moment. In the last chapter, Phil Wilson talked about a study (Greater Glasgow Health Board 1994) where young people described how matters like embarrassment and worries about confidentiality can make it difficult to seek help from their doctor.

Imagine for the moment that the voices of this small group were echoed by young people as a whole (not a claim the study makes). Would those of us who are involved in helping young people be surprised at this? Would we view their concerns as reasonable? If they were being taken seriously, how might this affect the way we plan and offer services? For example, have we ensured that we have particular skills to help young people manage their embarrassment? Are young women offered the opportunity to opt for a female worker? What is confidential and what must be passed on? Hearing these voices and respond-ing to them could make a useful contribution to enabling young people make the step of going for help.

Asking for help is an important step towards getting help – already there is an achievement to be recognised and acknowledged. Thinking about the young person making the journey into helping settings as something of a refugee can serve to remind us both of their vulnerability and their achievement. They're going somewhere they would rather not go, into a role around which prejudice is rife, and all at a time when their own resources are low.

This raises some important questions for the person who is there when a young person comes looking for help. Here is a young person in difficulty, yet she or he is innovating – doing a new thing. When did I last do that? Do I see this as an achievement? Is it important? How do I acknowledge it? Alongside the knowledge that the professional person has about the young person's 'problem' there needs to be a capacity to recognise these matters and acknowledge their importance for the young person.

The place of parents

Howie Feel tells us that young people can talk more readily to their friends than to their parents about how they feel. They may also find talking to doctors difficult (Greater Glasgow Health Board 1994). Yet most young people do go to doctors and most of them go along with their Mums. (Some go alone, very few go with Dads or friends.) Why is this? Where do parents fit in the picture?

Neither study can tell us that. Perhaps the young person has had no real opportunity to choose. Another possibility is that when a young person is in difficulty, the involvement of parents takes on a different meaning: their involvement becomes 'OK' or even welcome. Young people and parents can tell us more about this.

There are several issues which I've found in meeting and working with young people. First, as they become older, more young people choose to be seen on their own. Second, there is considerable variety between cultures (and sub-cultures) about what young people are expected or permitted to do for themselves. Third, the particular problem may influence what happens. So, for example, whilst there are services for young people which seldom involve parents (e.g. ChildLine), there are those (e.g. psychiatric services) which would seldom work with (particularly younger) teenagers without the involvement of a parent.

Many agencies offering mental health services for young people work with both young people and parents. Parents can play an important role in helping to address the problem and, indeed, the problem affecting the young person's life often has a major effect on the lives of parents and other family members. However, there may be occasions where parents have concerns that they do not wish to voice in front of the young person or the young person may not wish to speak in front of their parent(s). Services should, therefore, be clear about these important matters and whose interests are served by their policy.

What should professional services be doing about young people's mental health?

Services for young people need to be active in three areas:

- responding to concerns and problems

- raising discussion on issues that bear on mental health, for example lifestyle, sexual behaviour, relationships

- raising awareness of problems which are hidden, for example abuse, bullying, prejudice.

There are numerous examples of good practice in all of these areas, not only in mental health services (or indeed only in health services) but throughout the whole network of those involved with young people. There should be no illusion that all the skills necessary to support young people and to respond to their needs are located within any one place; rather, these skills are widespread among those who work closely with young people.

There are, however, particular tasks – for example, counselling a young woman who has been sexually abused, helping a young man who has developed a mental illness, such as schizophrenia, or working with the family of an adopted young person – where special skill and experience is needed. The key to good services for young people is establishing a network with a *range* of services which can change and adapt as the needs of young people change.

The way help is organised and offered

When characterising services for young people, there are a few issues that should be considered in all areas of work, everyday or specialised:

- young people are entitled to health care as a *right*; it is not a privilege

- young people are entitled to expect that the values of their culture will be *respected* within the services offered to them

- helping services should ensure that they are *accessible* to the young people who may wish to consult them

- helping services should ask those who consult them what *they* think about their services.

A Health Advisory Service document (NHS 1995) reaches a major conclusion about mental health services for children and young people in England and Wales (and we now know the findings hold true for Scotland). It said that while the services for the mental health needs of the young population were often of good quality, they were often poorly planned and uncoordinated. They said that the different agencies needed to co-operate. This would involve making sure that their plans for young people's services were in tune with each other and, where possible, services would collaborate to meet the needs of the young population. They thought this issue so important that they called the report *Together We Stand.*

While that document goes on to give lots of good idea about services, it makes it clear that people need to get together to work out how this is to be done in each area. This involves a number of steps:

- building up a current picture of young people's needs
- getting a good description of what is already available
- naming the strengths, weaknesses and gaps
- working out possible ways of tackling unmet need
- counting what this means by way of resources
- deciding on priorities
- monitoring any new developments.

Organisations such as health boards, local authorities, voluntary agencies and others need to meet and try to go through these steps together. Where agencies can agree together general priorities, it may become possible to develop shared projects. For instance, young people who find themselves being looked after in children's centres often have many difficulties – in relationships, with learning, with how they view themselves. Mental health services and local authority social work services might think together about how to meet the mental health needs of this vulnerable group.

Adapting to new demands and new voices is often difficult. Organisations, like individuals, can find it easier to replicate old patterns rather than innovate. However, there are good examples of health and other agencies responding creatively to these challenges. This *How We Feel* book is one such example – bringing together the voices of young people and those who work with them.

More challenges and dilemmas

As we look at the range of influences on services for young people, the voice of Howie Feel may begin to seem faint and difficult to recognise. This is one of the dilemmas for professionals working in these services at present.

As recently as twenty years ago there were very few health services specially designed for young people. Mental health services led the way and other medical services are now developing young people's services. However, this is a fairly new professional area and the people who work in these services sometimes struggle, like the young people they work with, to have their 'voice' heard and their concerns respected.

It is important to acknowledge that the task of meeting and supporting young people in distress can be difficult for those involved. Proper training, adequate resources and good support go a long way towards offsetting these pressures. At times, too, the task is rewarding in itself and a young person finds the help offered allows them to get on with her or his life again. However, there are some situations where options for change are difficult to recognise and the practitioner spends time 'standing by' the young person, helping them to maintain hope. It is important that practitioners make their own voices heard at those times, so that they can experience the support of colleagues. Like everyone else, professionals need ways of supporting and maintaining their own mental health.

Given all of these circumstances, it is not unusual (and maybe not surprising) to find what has been described recently as a 'professional bubble' (Reimers and Treacher 1995) – a distance between practitioners and the people who consult them. Perhaps those who consult these services have a part to play in bursting that bubble!

So what do good services look like?

They are well organised:

- ° they identify communities who may be particularly in need or able to benefit from those services

- ° they identify those communities likely to experience difficulty accessing services

- ° they develop strategy in relation to service provision.

They understand their task:

- ° they are clear about their strengths and weaknesses

- ° they are clear about the limits of what they can do

- ° they review the use of services, particularly aiming to identify the patterns of use and 'underuse'

- ° they are interested in developing and adapting to changing demand.

They are open to the young people who consult them:

- ° they recognise the 'developmental agenda' around for their young client group: family relationships, education and work, lifestyle and health

- ○ they respect the young people as individuals
- ○ they're interested in what the young people who consult them think of the services.

They are professional:

- ○ they are concerned to learn from their own and others' experience
- ○ they ensure that their staff are appropriately skilled, supervised and supported
- ○ they expect the respect of others in so far as the work they do is good work
- ○ they see themselves as accountable to those who consult them as well as those who employ them
- ○ they are prepared to act as advocates for their young client group.

Conclusion

Organising and offering services for young people is a complex task and those involved face many demands. *How We Feel* adds some new voices to this discussion, inviting us to recognise the experiences of young people themselves. It encourages us to work with young people and not just for them. It also encourages us to create and develop with them opportunities to influence the organisation and delivery of services at every stage.

The dilemma about using outside help is likely to remain as long as young people, like the rest of us, find the task of entrusting personal matters to a newcomer a bit daunting. However, it may be that as we become better at hearing the voices of young people, the leap in the dark that is often expected of those needing help can become a simpler step.

Methodology

Our aim was to obtain a snapshot of the feelings and emotional health of mid-adolescent girls and boys in Glasgow. We therefore designated the 25th October 1995 as 'Howie Feel Day' – a day during Scottish Mental Health Week when young people would be given the opportunity to tell us how they feel.

We felt that an expedient way to capture teenagers' experiences was to approach secondary schools and ask them to administer questionnaires to their third year pupils who in turn would complete these on an anonymous basis; pupils in third year are likely to be aged between thirteen-and-a-half and fourteen-and-a-half years old.

We developed our questionnaire, and piloted it on a number of occasions to ensure that teenagers experienced no difficulties in completing it. Several considerations guided its design. We felt that the questionnaire should be straightforward and appealing to teenagers with differing levels of academic ability; that they should be non-intrusive and allow respondents to gauge for themselves the degree of personal details which they choose to divulge; and that it should balance the twin aims of being exploratory in nature, but should be rooted in what we already know about mental health. For the latter reason, some questions aimed to identify sources of self-esteem and sources of emotional/social support – both of which reduce the vulnerability of children and adolescents developing mental health problems. (We have included a copy of the questionnaire in Appendix 2).

We aimed to paint a picture of adolescent feelings spanning the socio-economic spectrum. Our first step then was in securing approval from the Strathclyde Regional Council Department of Education, (and subsequently at a divisional level) for us to invite twenty schools citywide, to participate in our survey. In addition to this, we approached seven independent schools.

Thirteen state schools and three independent ones agreed to participate, representing a total of 2486 Secondary 3 pupils. For those pupils attending state schools, we were required to obtain parental approval using a standard 'opt-in' form. Partly for this reason, and partly because we wanted teenagers to develop a positive attitude to the whole concept of Howie Feel Day, we produced a range of promotional materials (posters, scratchcards and T-shirts) which were distributed in the two weeks leading up to the event.

On Howie Feel Day, teachers were provided with written explanatory notes and instructions which they were asked to read to the pupils, prior to them completing their questionnaires. The teenagers were assured of the anonymity of their responses, and informed that their questionnaires would be sent straight to the Health Board unread by school staff. To this end, they were issued blank envelopes on which they were to write only their gender. Once they had completed their questionnaires, respondents were requested to put them into the envelopes, seal them, hand them to the teacher who in turn would pass the envelopes unopened to the Health Board.

Of the 2486 teenagers targeted, 1634 completed questionnaires. This represents an overall response rate of 66 per cent.

HOWIE FEEL

health
PROMOTION
DEPARTMENT

Sometimes adults do not know how it really feels to be your age. On these pages we are asking you questions about how you feel. There are no right or wrong answers because we are all different. You do not need to put your name on the paper. We just want you to think carefully about each question and answer them all.

Here are lots of words which describe different kinds of feelings. Please draw a circle around each word which describes how you are feeling today.

---

coping   laid back   trapped   chirpy   not coping

energetic   confused   bored   tense   useless

happy   bad about the future   cheerful   lively   sensitive

pleased   angry   lonely   confident   disappointed

brave

fine   stressed   smug   important

romantic   scared   jealous   depressed   bitter   lucky

shy   ashamed   loved   calm   strong

failure   successful   on top of the world   frustrated

unconfident   fed up

frightened   good about the future   pleased with myself

HOWIE FEEL
- page 2 -

THREE things which make me feel happy are:

THREE things which make me feel unhappy are:

THREE things which make me feel *good* about myself are:

THREE things which make me feel *bad* about myself are:

HOWIE FEEL
- page 3 -

Howie Feel

I can talk about my feelings to:
(You can give more than one answer here)

If I felt bad I would:

When I feel bad, I would like it if:
(Think about who you would want to help you, and how)

HOWIE FEEL
- page 4 -

How I feel today

*(We want you to think very carefully about <u>how it feels to be you today</u>. We have
left you a lot of space for you to do this. Imagine that you are writing your own
diary, and say exactly how you feel.*

Dear Diary

Thank you very much for doing this.

References

Brown, G.W. and Harris, T.O. (1978) *Social Origins of Depression: A Study of Psychiatric Disorder in Women.* London: Tavistock.

Coleman, J.C. and Hendry, L. (1990) *The Nature of Adolescence.* London: Routledge.

Coles, R. and Stokes, G. (1985) *Sex and the American Teenager.* New York: Harper and Row.

Coopersmith, S. (1967) *The Antecedents of Self-Esteem.* San Francisco: Freeman.

Csikszentmihalyi, M. and Larson, R. (1984) *Being Adolescent: Conflict and Growth in the Teenage Years.* New York: Basic Books.

Cvetkovich, G. and Grote, B. (1980) 'Psychological development and the social program of teenage illegitimacy.' In C. Chilman (ed) *Adolescent Pregnancy and Childbearing: Findings from Research.* Washington, DC: US Department of Health and Human Services.

Epstein, S. (1973) 'The self-concept revisited or a theory of a theory.' *American Psychologist 28,* 404–416.

Fine, L. (1977) *After All We've Done For Them.* Englewood Cliffs, NJ: Prentice Hall.

Graham, H. (1994) 'Gender and class as dimensions of smoking behaviour in Britain: insights from a survey of mothers.' *Social Science and Medicine 38,* 5, 691–698.

Graham, P. and Hughes, C. (1995) *So Young, So Sad, So Listen.* London: Gaskell.

Greater Glasgow Health Board (1994) *The Doctor and You: Report on Pilot Survey into Uptake of Health Services in Cambuslang.* Unpublished paper: Health Promotion Department, Greater Glasgow Health Board.

Greater Glasgow Health Board (1996) *Drugs and Alcohol: A Prevalence Study among 12–15-year-olds in Greater Glasgow 1996.* Greater Glasgow Health Board, Health Promotion Department.

Hall, J. (1996) *Stressed Out – What children tell ChildLine about Exams and Work Pressure.* London: ChildLine.

Harter, S. (1983) 'The development of the self-esteem.' In M. Hetherington (ed) *Handbook of Child Psychology: Social and Personality Development.* New York: Wiley.

Hill, M., Laybourn, A. and Borland, M. (1996a) *Children's Wellbeing.* Centre for the Study of the Child and Society, University of Glasgow.

Hill, M., Laybourn, A., Borland, M. and Secker, J. (1996b) 'Promoting mental and emotional well-being: the perceptions of younger children.' In D.R. Trent (ed) *Promoting Mental Health Volume 5.* Aldershot: Avebury.

Jones, W.H. (1981) 'Loneliness and social contact.' *Journal of Psychology 113,* 295–296.

MacLeod, M. (1996) *We Know it's Tough to Talk: Boys in Need of Help.* London: ChildLine.

MacLeod, M. and Morris, S. (1996) *Why Me? – Children Talking to ChildLine about Bullying.* London: ChildLine.

NHS Health Advisory Service (1995) *Together We Stand: The Commissioning, Role and Management of Child and Adolescent Mental Health Services.* London: HMSO.

Offer, D., Ostrov, E. and Howard, K. (1981) *The Adolescent: A Psychological Portrait.* New York: Basic Books.

Pavis, S., Masters, H. and Cunningham-Burley, S. (1996) *Lay Concepts of Positive Mental Health and How it Can be Maintained.* Department of Public Health Sciences, University of Edinburgh.

Reimers, S. and Treacher, A. (1995) *Introducing User Friendly Family Therapy.* London: Routledge.

Rogers, C.R. (1983) *Freedom To Learn for the 80s.* Oxford:Maxwell MacMillan International Publishing Group.

Rutter, M. (1983) 'School effects on pupils' progress: research findings and policy implications.' *Child Development 54,* 1–29.

Rylance, G., Bowen, C. and Rylance, J. (1995) 'Measles and rubella immunisation: information and consent in children.' *British Medical Journal 311,* 923–924.

Savin-Williams, R.C. and Berndt, T. (1990) 'Friendship and peer relations.' In S.S. Feldman and G.R. Elliott (eds) *At The Threshold: The Developing Adolescent.* London: Harvard University Press.

Scottish Central Committee on Guidance (1986) *More Than Feelings Of Concern.* Dundee College of Education for the Consultative Committee on the Curriculum. Glasgow: Russell Print.

Steinberg, L. (1987) 'The impact of puberty on family relations: effects of pubertal status and pubertal timing.' *Developmental Psychology 23,* 451–460.

Steinberg, L. (1988) 'Reciprocal relation between parent–child distance and pubertal maturation.' *Developmental Psychology 24,* 122–128.

Sullivan, H.S. (1953) *The Interpersonal Theory of Psychiatry.* New York: Norton.

West, P. and Sweeting, H. (1996) 'Nae jobs, nae future: young people and health in a context of unemployment.' *Health and Social Care in the Community 4,* 1, 50–62.

Youniss, J. and Smollar, J. (1985) *Adolescents' Relations with Mothers, Fathers and Friends.* Chicago: University of Chicago Press.

The Contributors

Graham Bryce is a Consultant Child and Adolescent Psychiatrist, with a particular interest in the planning and organisation of services, at the Possilpark Health Centre, Glasgow.

Sally Butler is a Consultant Clinical Psychologist, with a particular interest in child and adolescent health and the prevention of mental health problems, at the Royal Hospital for Sick Children, Glasgow

Jacki Gordon is Senior Health Promotion Officer for Mental Health, Greater Glasgow Health Board.

Gillian Grant is a Health Promotion Officer for Youth, Greater Glasgow Health Board.

Anne Houston is the Director of ChildLine Scotland.

Susan McGinnis is a counsellor, with a particular interest in young people, at the University of Strathclyde, Glasgow.

George Potter is a principal teacher of guidance, and a person-centred therapist, at Cathkin High School, Glasgow.

Sister Mary Ross is an educational psychologist and Director of the Notre Dame Child Guidance Clinic and Adolescent Unit, Glasgow.

Dr Jenny Secker was at the time of writing the Specialist Research and Evaluation Officer (Mental Health and Special Needs) for the Health Education Board for Scotland and is now a Senior Research Fellow at the Centre for Mental Health Services Development, King's College, London.

Dr Carol Tannahill is Director of Health Promotion, Greater Glasgow Health Board.

Peter Wilson is a child psychotherapist and the Director of Young Minds, the children's mental health charity.

Dr Phil Wilson is a General Practitioner and Research Fellow with the Department of General Practice, University of Glasgow.

Subject
Index

Author Index